BERMUDA IN FULL COLOR

Hans W. Hannau
With revisions by William Zuill

BERMUDA
in full color

NEWLY REVISED EDITION
With 92 Color Photographs

Macmillan Press Ltd / Bermuda Bookstore Ltd

This edition published 1994

Published by THE MACMILLAN PRESS LTD
London and Basingstoke
*Associated companies and representatives in Accra,
Auckland, Delhi, Dublin, Gaborone, Hamburg, Harare,
Hong Kong, Kuala Lumpur, Lagos, Manzini, Melbourne,
Mexico City, Nairobi, New York, Singapore, Tokyo.*

ISBN 0–333–57060–X

Printed in Hong Kong

A catalogue record for this book is available from the
British Library.

The authors and publishers acknowledge with thanks the following
photographic sources:
Bermuda National Trust (p61)
Government Information Services (p34)
M Emmerson (front cover, pp26, 76 top)
Princess Hotels International Ltd (p41 top)
Marriott's Castle Harbour Hotel (p86 bottom)
All other photographs are courtesy of the author.
The publishers have made every effort to trace the copyright
holders but if they have overlooked any, they will be pleased
to make the necessary arrangements at the first opportunity.

DISTRIBUTED in BERMUDA by BERMUDA BOOKSTORE-BAXTERS LTD

INTRODUCTION

Bermuda has created a style of architecture, a style of dress, and a style of life. The island is not one but about 138 islands, large and small. Altogether they comprise a little more than twenty square miles. Visiting Bermuda is rather like visiting a South Sea island in the North Atlantic. It is also rather like vacationing on a luxurious cruise ship. Though the islands are in the blue North Atlantic, palm trees grow there and it never snows or freezes. The people don't wear grass skirts there, but the islands have inspired Bermuda shorts, a symbol of informality. Bermuda has its own style of architecture, represented by delightful houses with steep white roofs and with walls that are either white or tinted pastel. These island houses, literally cut from the rock, are now influencing the residential architecture of tropical and subtropical resorts thousands of miles away.

Bermuda is the first great modern resort island in the Atlantic and Caribbean area. It has perfected the art of being kind to strangers over many generations — indeed, since shipwrecked colonists came ashore in 1609. It has never forgotten the gallant seafarers who made it the greatest training ground for sailors the world has ever known, even greater than the home of the forefathers of the first Bermudians, England. Bermuda sloops were the fastest in the world in the great days of sail.

Bermuda is a land of contrasts. The fragrance of roses and lilies is laced with salt air. Though more than 600,000 visitors come to the islands annually, there still are lonely and magnificent coves where a solitary can find peace. The most modern amenities are found in the many fine hotels, clubs, and cottage colonies. Here also are small streets winding through a seventeenth-century set-

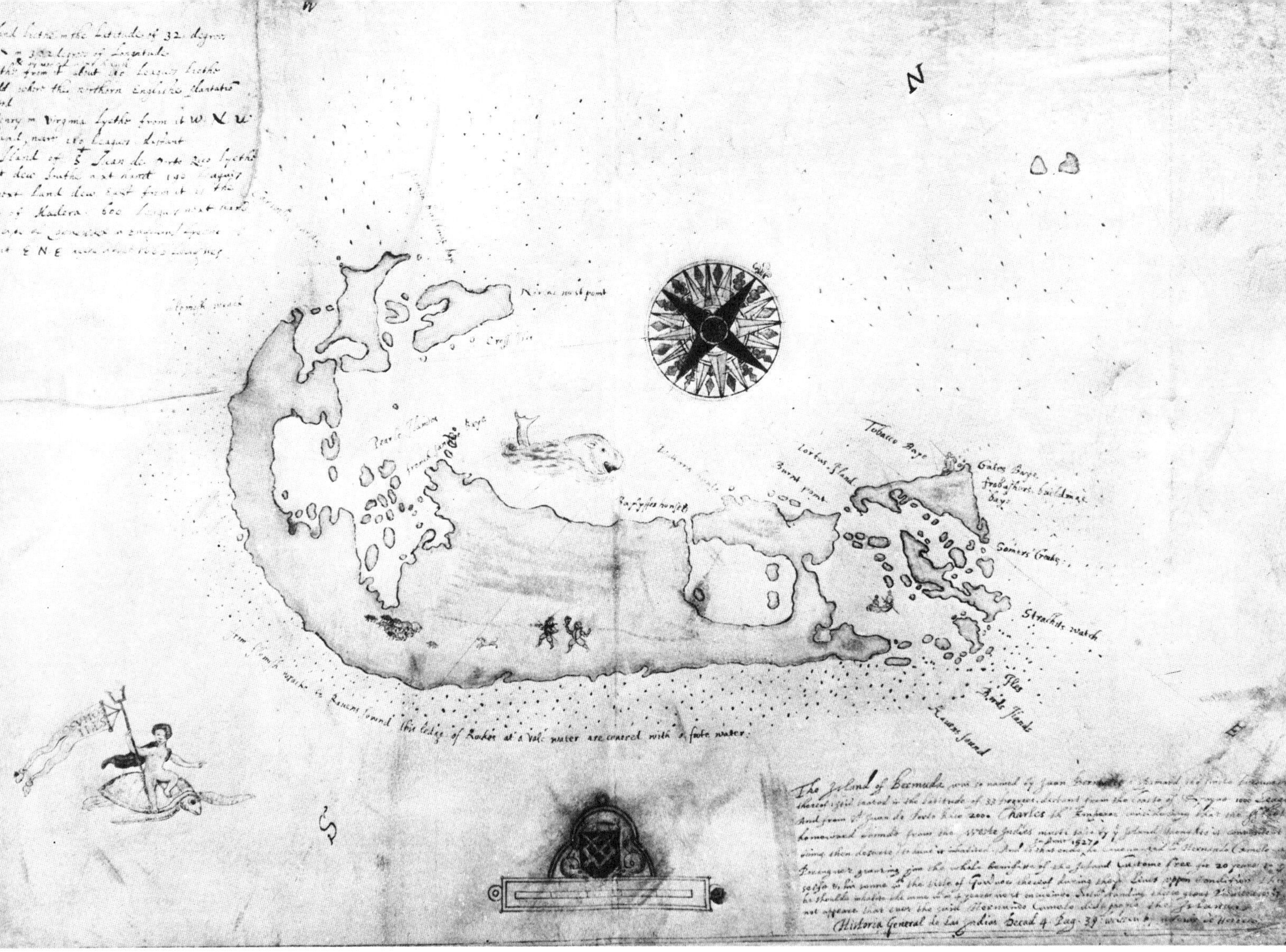

Sir George Somers' Map of Bermuda

tlement, and old forts built to defend against the Spanish and the French.

Golfing, tennis, swimming, searching for sunken treasure are only a few of the pleasures Bermuda offers. In addition to exploring the beaches and the looping coves and sounds along the shores, one can explore underground, for nowhere in the world are there more magnificent big caverns per acre. Many are lighted to allow the public to enjoy their beauty. Diving down to the colorful gardens of the coral reefs that surround Bermuda is an unforgettable experience. Bermuda was the base for the Sea Lab experiment, in which men camped beneath the sea.

The climate, which is idyllic, draws people to Bermuda where winter never comes. The serene pace of life on the islands and the wide variety of ways to rest and relax bring visitors back again and again.

HISTORY

Bermuda emerges into history with a reputation for being enchanted and mysterious. A Spanish seafarer, Juan de Bermúdez, gave his name to the isolated group of little islands in the mid-Atlantic. He sailed by them or was wrecked upon them, and the date of his discovery was in 1505/6, according to the most recent researches. On a map of the Atlantic and its islands in Peter Martyr's **Legatio Babylonica,** published in 1511, "La Bermuda" was shown. On a high cliff called Spanish Rock on the south shore is cut a cross, the letters "T" and "F" now almost worn away, and the date 1543. Their origin is unknown. An English sea captain, Henry May, was wrecked here in 1593, and when he returned to England he gave an account of the islands.

The reefs round Bermuda were probably responsible for the wreckage of other adventurers of the sixteenth century, for in Queen Elizabeth's time the islands had achieved a reputation for being devil-haunted, mysterious, evil, and enchanted. Navigators avoided them like the plague. It was therefore a grand surprise to the shipwrecked party that landed in 1609 to find that they were lovely islands, with herds of wild pigs, fine cedar timber, nourishing plants, and a delightful, frostfree climate.

The landing was hair-raising. In that year a fleet loaded with food, other supplies, and colonists was sent out to bring relief to Jamestown, England's first settlement in America. The admiral of the fleet was Sir George Somers, who began his seafaring career as a buccaneer, acquiring wealth and knighthood through the Spanish prizes he captured.

The Virginia Company put him in command of a relief fleet of seven tall ships and two pinnaces. His 300-ton flagship, the **Sea Venture,** was the largest ship that sailed from Plymouth to aid Jamestown.

THE TEMPEST

The storm that struck the fleet is immortalized in Shakespeare's **The Tempest.** After seven weeks at sea, the **Sea Venture** lost sight of the rest of the fleet. The winds howled for three days and nights, and the ship, leaking heavily, had nearly sunk when land was sighted on the morning of July 28, 1609. Sir George steered his ship toward shore, for though he recognized that the land must be the devil-haunted Bermudas, devils were to be preferred to storms at that point. An account of the adventures of those men, women, and children shipwrecked on Bermuda was written by William Strachey, the secretary-elect of Virginia, and was later widely read in England. It is considered that this story inspired Shakespeare.

Strachey wrote: "... a dreadfull storme and hideous began to blow from out the north-east, which swelling, and roaring as it were by fits, some houres with more violence than others, at length did beat all light from heaven, which like a hell of darkenesse turned blacke upon us, so much the fuller of horror ... surely as death comes not so elvish and painfull as at sea ... our clamours dround in the windes, and the windes in thunder ... The sea swelled above the clouds, and gave battell unto Heaven. It could not be said to raine, the waters like whole rivers did flood in the ayre. The glut of water was no sooner a little emptied and qualified, but instantly the windes (as having gotten their mouths now free, and at liberty) spake more loud, and grew more tumultuous and malignant."

The seams of the **Sea Venture** opened and everyone took turns working the pumps and bailing with buckets, including Admiral Somers and the Governor, Lord De la Warr. Finally the ship crunched between two rocks and was fast lodged and locked. The hundred and fifty men, women, and children were taken to shore in the long-boat and skiff, and they found themselves on "the dreaded islands of Bermuda ... called commonly the Devils Islands [which] are feared and avoided of all sea travellers alive, above any other place in the world," according to Strachey. The spot where the ship went aground off the eastern end of Bermuda is called Sea Venture Flat. Sir Thomas Gates was in the first boat-load of survivors to reach the shore, and he named the spot where they landed Gates' Bay.

Portrait of Sir George Somers by Van Somer

THE WEALTH OF BERMUDA

They found on the dreaded islands a wealth of food and beauty. Strachey wrote that Admiral Somers took so many fish in half an hour that they sufficed the whole company for one day.

"The fish are so good as these parts of the world afford not the like; which being for the most part unknown to us, each man gave them names as they best liked. As one kind they called rock fish, another groopers, others porgy fish, hogge fish, angel fish, cavallyes, yellow tayles, Spanish makarell, mullets, breame, conny fish, morrayers, sting tayles, flying fish, &c."

Many of those fish bear the same names today.

Further describing what substituted for manna in this hospitable and beautiful wilderness, Strachey wrote: "But above all these, most deservinge of observation are two sortes of birdes, the one (from the tune of his voice), the other (from the effect), called the cahowe and the egg bird, the latter arriving constantly on May 1, falls a layinge infinite stores of egges, upon certaine small sandy islands and so continue all that monthe, being all the while so tame and fearelesse that they suffer themselves to be thrust

off their eggs: so that many thousands of egges (being as bigge as hens' egges) were eaten. The cahowe (for so sounded his voice) all the summer we saw not, and in the darkest nights of November and December (for in the night they onely feed) they would come forth, but not flye farre, making a strange hollow and harsh howling. These birds for their blindness (for they see weakly in the day) and for their cry, wee called the sea owle — wee caught them with a light bough in a darke night. Our men found a prettie way to take them which was by hollowing and laughing, with the noise thereof, the birds would come flocking and settle upon the very arms of him that so cryed: by which our men would weigh them and which weighed the heaviest they tooke, twentie dozen in two hours."

As if fish and eggs were not sufficient, "There were wilde hogges upon the island. Our people would go a hunting with our ship dogge, and sometimes bring home thirtie boares, sowes and pigs in a weeke alive. From August and November they were well fed with berries that dropped from the cedars and palm but in February when the palm berries were scant and the cedar ber-

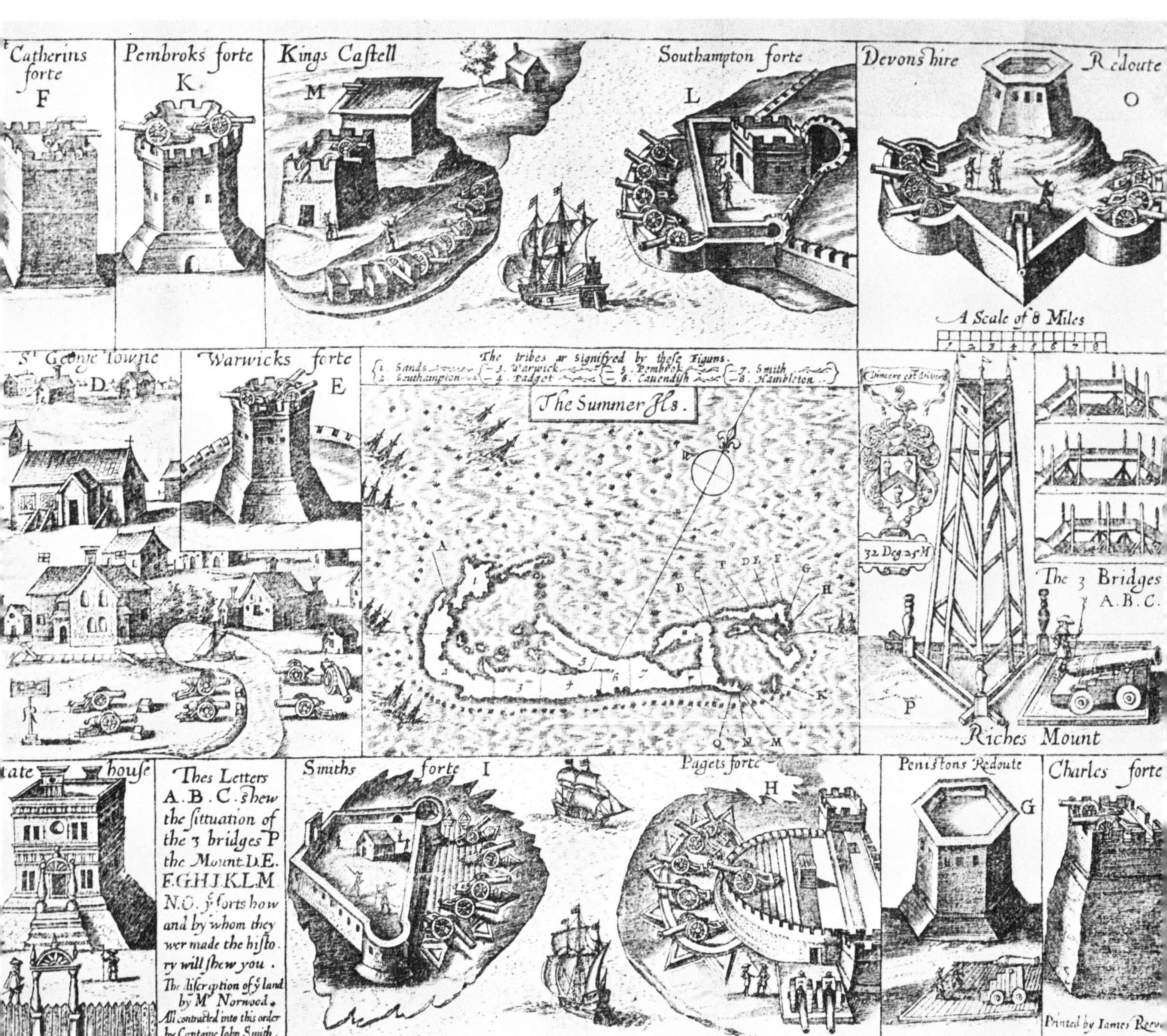

Engraving of Bermuda's forts as they were between 1612 and 1615, as they appear in Capt. John Smith's works

ries had failed two monthes sooner, true it is the hogges grew poore."

It is speculated that these hogs were descendants of a cargo of hogs that were being carried to Cuba by Juan de Bermúdez more than a century before when he was wrecked on the islands to which he gave his name.

When the hogs grew poor, "then the tortoyses came in. Their meat is such as a man can neither absolutely call fish nor flesh, keeping most in the water and feeding upon sea-grasse like a heifer."

They roasted the heart of the sabal palms, called cabbage palms in Florida, and used the leaves to thatch their cabins. It wasn't unalloyed bliss, though, for they did find prickle pears and poison ivy, which caused redness, itching, and blisters. There was no venomous creature on the Bermudas, and no human living there.

Those men, women, and children who had been going out to colonize Virginia set to work, under the direction of Admiral Somers, not only to keep alive but also to build ships, and they started a great tradition of ship-building on Bermuda. They put up rough shelters thatched with palm fronds. They mapped the string of islands, shaped like a fish-hook. A long boat was built and set sail to find aid for the marooned group. It was never seen again. Two other ships were built. A couple was wed, a man was killed, children were born during the nine months before the group finally sailed for Jamestown. What they found there was not nearly as good as what they had left in Bermuda, for famine and Indians had reduced the Jamestown colony to sixty people. They went back to Bermuda to get more food, and there Admiral Sir George Somers, a hard-working and able man, died on November 8, 1610. The island on which he died is called St. George's.

The First Permanent Settlement

The group sailed for England, leaving on Bermuda only three renegades. Thrilled by the tales the survivors brought home, the Virginia Company obtained the grant of the Bermudas from James I and in 1612 sent out the first permanent settlers, sixty people with ship's carpenter Richard Moore as governor. This was eight years before the Pilgrims landed at Plymouth Rock. Governor Moore inspired the colonists to build wharves for shipping and small forts to defend the islands against possible Spanish raids. They planted tobacco, corn, wheat, beans, and melons. A treasure of ambergris found on the shore was sent to England.

The colony was declining in energy when

Inscription on Spanish Rock

Bermuda was taken over by the Somers' Island Company under a new charter in 1615, and energetic Daniel Tucker was sent out as governor with new settlers. He is immortalized in a Mother Goose rhyme:

"Ole Dan Tucker was a funny old man,
He washed his face in a frying pan,
He combed his hair with a wagon wheel
And died with a toothache in his heel."

His successor, Governor Nathaniel Butler, introduced parliamentary government to Bermuda, and the first General Assembly, which made local laws, was held on August 1, 1620. Bermuda's Parliament is the oldest in the British Commonwealth.

In the 1620s, spurred by Governor Butler, bridges were built between the main islands. Also a fort, a church, and a Sessions House were erected at St. George's, the capital town. In the building of the Sessions House a mortar made of lime and turtle oil was used to bind the limestone walls. It still stands, the oldest building in Bermuda.

A specially fitted ship was sent out from England to catch whales, and whaling became for a long time an important item in the Bermudian economy.

At this time Bermuda got its first coins, to replace the bartering that had been the way of trade in the islands. The coins had a hog on one side, to honor the wild hogs that had fed the first shipwrecked colonists, and the coins became known as "Hog Money." They were of copper.

Slavery in Bermuda

The first slaves, one Indian and one Negro, were brought to Bermuda in 1616 to dive for pearls. Slavery soon came to be a way of life. Many more Negroes were brought from the West Indies, and some Indians from the English colonies in North America. Soon Bermuda had too many slaves. Because sugar cane, which needs much strong, cheap labor, was not so exten-sively grown in Bermuda as it was in the West Indies, there was not a real economic need for slavery. In the seventeenth and eighteenth centuries the majority of slaves were servants. There were several slave revolts on Bermuda, as in the other British colonies, and they were repressed with unspeakable cruelty. There were periods when the only fresh meat the slaves ever got was

The Description of the Sommer Ilands, once
called the BERMVDAS.

AS it hath pleased God of his especiall grace and mercy to deliuer this Nation from that sinke of errours, and superstitious practises wherewith the face of Christendome was ouerspread : and hath caused the truth of Pietie and Religion to shine amongst vs, through the effectuall Ministry of his Word : In so much that there is no Nation in the world, to whom the grace of God hath (in these latter times) more abounded, nor where true Religion hath beene so generally imbraced and maintained, as in this Kingdome : So hath he likewise deliuered vs from many eminent dangers, and euill practises at home and abroad : hath blessed vs with much peace and prosperitie : and moreouer, hath honoured vs with such notable fauours, that the fame of the worthy exploits, and noble attempts of this Nation by Sea and by Land, hath resounded to the glory of his Name, euen to the farthest parts of the earth ; And I beseech God (in the name of him in whom alone he is well-pleased) still to continue this his goodnesse towards vs, although in these times we haue iust cause to feare the contrary.

Amongst these latter sort of Benefits which God hath vouchsafed to this Nation, I meane that magnanimitie and courage, and his diuine assistance in the prosecution of so many notable actions, may worthily, in my iudgement (though sleighted at by some) be reckoned that noble enterprise, of planting VIRGINIA with Christian Religion, and Engiish people. And as he hath manifested his succour and prouidence many wayes, beyond expectation, for the aduancement of this worke, so not a little in the discouery of the Sommer Ilands : for, (to omit other reasons) these are as it were the Key, opening a passage, and making the way more safe to many parts of this new World, and especially to Virginia : so that if they had beene discouered and inhabited by any such as would oppose the planting of Virginia : It had proued a matter so difficult and dangerous, that in all likelihood it had beene relinquished ere this time ; of these I haue exhibited this description, with the relation following.

These Ilands, formerly called the Bermudas, now the Sommer Ilands, shunned by Trauellers, as most dangerous, and seldome seene by any, except against their wills ; reputed to be rather a hold and habitation of Diuels, then any fit place for men to abide in, were discouered in the yeare 1609. in manner following. There was at that time eight Ships sent by the Aduenturers to Virginia, amongst which one of the best and strongest was called the Sea-venture, in burthen neare 300. tunne : In this, were their chiefe Commanders, Sir Thomas Gates, and Sir George Sommers, and with them about 150. persons. And vpon the 25. of Iuly the same yeare, being at Sea, this Ship called the Sea-venture, was by a fierce and terrible storme separated from the rest of the Fleete : and withall so shaken and torne by violence of the weather, that she sprung a leake : whereat the water came in so fast, that in short time it was seauen or eight foote deepe within the hold. Whereupon, for safetie of their shippe and liues, they fell to pumping, and bayling out the water with buckets ; and continued their labour for three dayes, and as many nights without intermission. But then perceiuing that they auailed nothing, the water in this space rather increasing, then any whit abating ; Now hopelesse of safetie, tyred and out-worne with labour, watching, and discomfort, and desirous to refresh their enfeebled spirits with some little rest before their death ; they resolued to ceasse their labour, and so by consequence permit their ship to sinke. Sir George Sommers sitting day and night all this while vpon the Poope, to direct the Shippe as euenly as might be, lest shee should be ouer-turned or swallowed of the waues, espied land, and thereupon called the Company together, and encouraged them againe to pumping, and casting out water, by which meanes they kept her vp from sinking, and by Gods prouidence escaped the rockes, till they gat within halfe a mile of the shoare, where shee stucke fast betweene two rockes. The extremitie of the storme being then well qualified, they had time to land all their men, most part of their prouision, and to saue much of their Ships tackling and Iron-worke before shee sanke. And thus it pleased God, by this euill, to bring to light a farre greater good, agreeable to that saying,

Qua latet, inq; bonis cessat non cognita rebus
Apparet vtrtus, arguiturq; malis.

Hauing thus escaped the eminent danger of present death, and all safely arriued : We may well conceiue their ioy to haue beene great, especially when they found there, in great abundance, Fish, Fowle, Hogs, and other things for the sustenance of man, and which they most of all feared, water : but no people, nor any kinde of Cattell, except those Hogges, and a few wilde Cats ; which in likelihood had swoom a-shore out of some Ship cast away vpon the coast, and there encreased. They abode there nine moneths, during which time, with helpe of such things as they saued of the Sea-venture, and of such as they found in the Countrey, they built of Cedar, and rigged fit for the Sea, two Vessels, a Ship and a Pinnace, and vpon the 10. of May 1610. departed toward Virginia, leauing onely two men behind them, and carrying with them store of prouision for the reliefe of the people there. Vpon the 24. of May, they arriued safely there, and shortly after some of them returned to the Sommer Ilands againe for a further supply, in the same Ship which they had formerly built there ; where Sir George Sommers dying, his men did not according to his last charge giuen vnto them, returne to Virginia ; but framed their course for England, leauing behinde them three men, that stayed voluntarily, who shortly after found in Sommerset Iland, which is part of Sandys Tribe, a very great treasure in Amber-greece, to the value of nine or ten thousand pound sterling : there hath also beene found since diuers times of the best sort.

This new discouery of the Sommer Ilands, being thus made knowne in England, to the Virginian Company, by these men which returned, they sold to some hundred and twentie persons of the same Company, who obtaind a Charter from his Majesty, and so hold it. And toward the latter end of Aprill, 1612. sent thither a Ship called the Plough, with some sixtie persons, to inhabite, appointing Gouernour one Master Richard Moore, a man ingenious and carefull, who since dyed in Sir Walter Rawleyes last voyage to Guiana, (a place as appeareth by our moderne Geographers, very rich and spatious.) But, as I say, he arriued there about the beginning of Iuly, and found the foresaid three men that stayed voluntarily, very well. Master Moore spent three yeares of his gouernment for the most part in fortifying the Country, and trayning the people in martiall exercises, which custome hath beene continued by his successours : he built some nine or tenne Forts, placing Ordnance and Munition in them. In his time, the Lord sent vpon the Countrey a very grieuous scourge and punishment, threatning the vtter ruine and desolation of it. That it came from God I neede not striue to proue, especially considering it was generally so acknowledged by vs at that time : The causes and occasions of it. I neede not name, being very well knowne to vs all that then liued there, which were about 600. persons, though shortly after much diminished. I will onely shew the thing it selfe, which was a wonderfull annoyance by silly Rattes : These Rattes comming at the first out of a Ship, few in number, increased in the space of two yeare, or lesse, so exceedingly, that they filled not onely those places where they were first landed : But swimming from place to place, spread themselues into all parts of the Countrey. In so much, that there was no Iland, though seuered by the Sea from all other Lands, and many miles distant from the Iles where the Rats had their originall but was pestered with them. They had their nests almost in euery tree, and in all places their Burrowes in the ground (like Connies) to harbour in. They spared not the fruits of plants or Trees, neither the Plants themselues, but eate them vp. When we had set our Corne, they would commonly come by troupes the night following, or so soone as it began to grow, and digge it vp againe. If by diligent watching any of it were preserued till it came to earing, it should then very hardly scape them. Yea, it was a difficult matter after we had it in our houses, to saue it from them, for they became noysome euen to the persons of men. Wee vsed all diligence for the destroying of them, nourishing many Cats, wilde and tame, for that purpose ; wee vsed Rats-bane, and many times set fire on the woods, so as the fire might runne halfe a mile or more before it were extinct : Euery man in the Countrey was enioyned to set twelue Traps, and some of their owne accord set neere a hundred, which they visited twice or thrice in a night. We trayned vp our Dogges to hunt them, wherein they grew so expert, that a good Dogge in two or three houres space, would kill fortie or fiftie Rattes, and other meanes we vsed to destroy them, but could not preuaile, finding them still to encrease against vs.

And this was the principall cause of that great distresse whereunto we were driuen in the first planting of the Country, for these, deuouring the fruits of the earth, kept vs destitute of bread a yeare, or two ; so that, when we had it afterwards againe, we were so weaned from it, that we should easily neglect and forget to eate it with our meate. We were also destitute at that time of Boats, and other prouision for Fishing. And moreouer, Master Moore had receiued warning from England, that he should

expect

whale meat. There was "no manner of work to employ them advantageously. But the inhabitants have a pride in keeping of them," reported one observer, describing slavery in Bermuda in the seventeenth century. He added, "No slaves in the West Indies are us'd so well as the Negroes are here." The Negroes made good and trustworthy crewmen on the wide-ranging Bermuda sailing ships. In many instances in Bermuda there was much mutual dependence and affection between whites and their black servants. Many of the Negroes became skilled in the building trades.

More and more, in England, men were denouncing slavery as vile. The beginning of the end came in England when in 1772 Lord Chief Justice Mansfield declared slavery to be "so odious that nothing could be suffered to support it but positive law." Since that positive law did not exist in England, slavery became illegal there after that decision, and 14,000 colored people gained their freedom.

What was acclaimed as "one of the greatest events in the history of mankind" came on July 31, 1834, when all slaves in British colonies were set free. Though the English Abolition Law provided for a six-year period of apprenticeship before complete freedom came, on Bermuda and Antigua all slaves were freed completely on August 1, 1834. Bermuda slave-owners received 128,340 pounds sterling in compensation.

Witchcraft and Superstitions

The witchcraft and superstitions of the West Indies are generally said to be African in origin. No such claim can be made as to the hysteria about witchcraft and the supernatural that prevailed in Bermuda for forty-six years, beginning with the arrival of Governor Josias Forster, who came in 1642 and encouraged the delusion. It came straight from England and northern Europe, which had been swept by this paranoid hysteria for years. King James I who commissioned the beautiful version of the Holy Bible that bears his name, believed thoroughly in witchcraft, wrote a book on the subject, and had laws passed providing hanging for witches. He has been called "the wisest fool in Christendom."

Many Scottish prisoners who had fought for Charles I against Cromwell were sent to Bermuda in 1651 and sold as slaves. Scotland was afire with the witch craze, and the Scots contaminated the Bermudians with their su-

Street Scene in old St. George's

perstitions. Governor Forster began the dreadful era of witch trials.

It was held that a witch, who had made a pact with the Devil, could not drown because water would reject her. The test of a witch was to tie her hands and feet together and throw her in the water. If she floated, she was a witch. This was known as "swimming a witch."

Old Jeanne Gardiner was so tested, and she floated and was hanged. She was the first of a series of men and women who were killed by neighbor's suspicions and talk. Witches and their male counterparts were accused of having the evil eye, of making psychic predictions and black magic, and of having a knowledge of magical herbs, potions, and poisons. It was not until the 1690s that this plague of the mind petered out, and the trials were discontinued. The witchcraft hysteria broke out in Salem, Massachusetts, in 1692.

Thereafter superstitions still prevailed in Bermuda, such as that a fabulous treasure was guarded by gnomes, that sudden squalls were raised by the devils. There is still belief in the supernatural and in the old folk-remedies, as there is just about everywhere. Some people in recent years have boasted of haunted houses and poltergeists.

The Bermuda Loyalists

When Oliver Cromwell led the Puritans to depose and behead King Charles I Bermudians were predominantly Loyalist and protested bitterly. They elected a governor to declare Charles II their king. They sent the Puritans in Bermuda away, and some of those Bermudians became the first English settlers of the Bahamas under the leadership of William Sayle. Though he had been Governor of Bermuda three times, he went to England and formed "The Company of Eleutherian Adventurers" to take his fellow Puritans away to a new land. Claiming that the Puritans were persecuted in Bermuda, he founded a colony on the Bahama island he named Eleuthera.

As a result of all this, Cromwell's English Parliament declared in 1650 that Bermuda was in a state of rebellion and forbade any trade with the colony so long as the rebellion went on. The colony had to knuckle under and to acknowledge Cromwell's Commonwealth, but all Bermuda celebrated when Charles II became King of England in 1660.

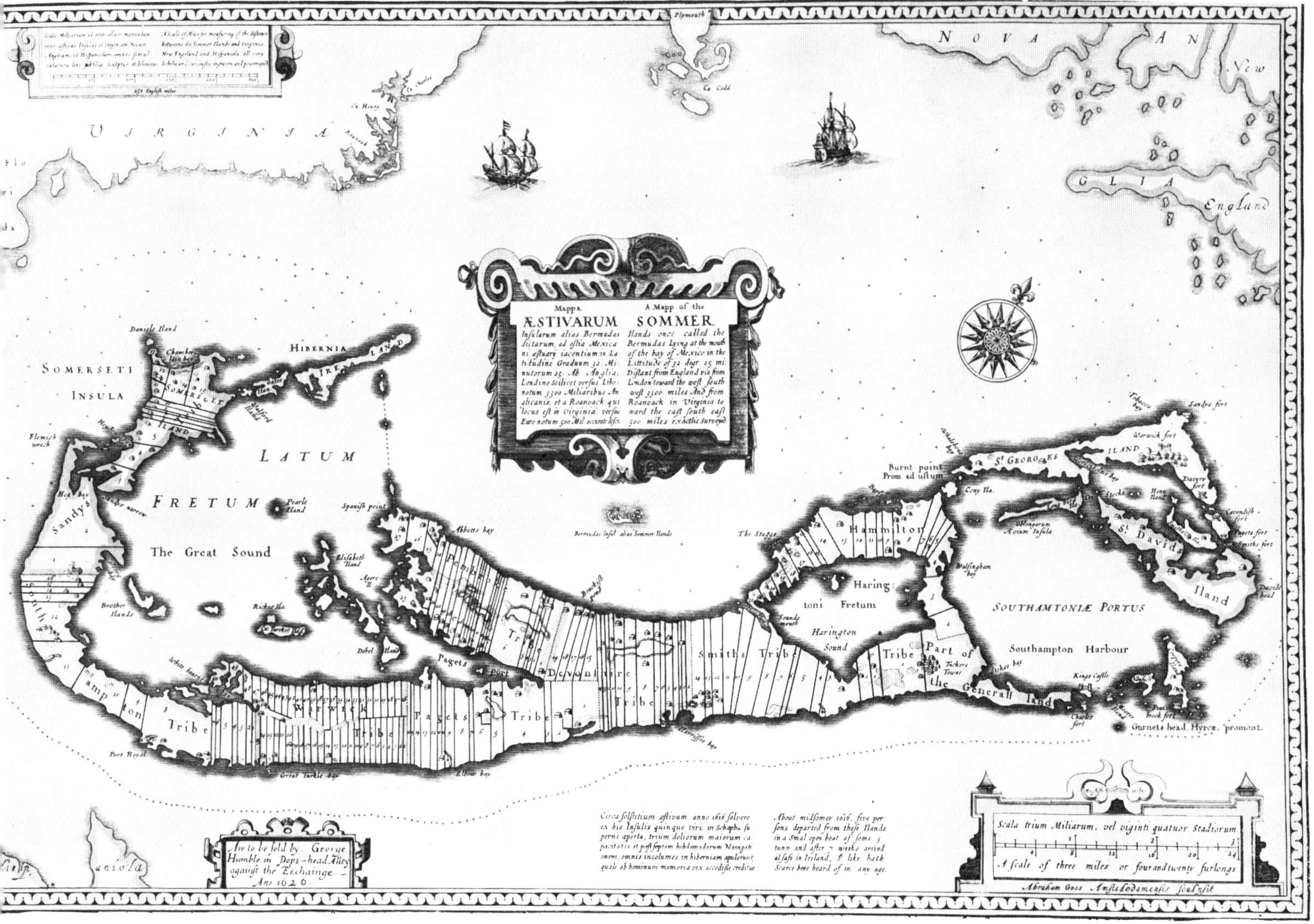

Richard Norwood's Map of 1622

Four Hundred Shares: Commissioned in 1618 to divide the British Colony of Bermuda into shares, Richard Norwood laid out 400 narrow strips. These shares were owned by the investors, who by common consent laid out "ye common paths to the sea" along the boundaries of every second share, thus creating 200 "tribe roads." This ancient map, which dates back to 1626, shows how the division was affected, and how the "tribe roads" ran in straight lines from shore to shore. Some present-day landowners claim they have found the axe-marks on rocks by the early settlers to get their bearings.

TURK'S ISLAND

Adventurous Bermuda seafarers, in the hard years of the latter half of the seventeenth century, decided to found a colony of their own. In 1668 they sailed south almost a thousand miles, to a small island of rocks and glistening sand. Here they came ashore and found no inhabitants. They called it Turk's Island, because they found there a cactus that looked like the head of a man wearing a fez.

On Turk's Island they built huge salt ponds and raked salt during the hot months from May to October. This hard, hot work was the mainstay of the Bermuda economy for more than a century, for salt was a valued article of trade.

Life on Bermuda was full of welcomes and good-bys for many families for a long, long time indeed. Bermudians on Turk's Island were carried off as prisoners by the French in 1763. In 1801, though the Bermudians protested bitterly, Turk's Island and its salt industry were made part of the Bahama colony.

Bermuda Becomes a Crown Colony

Toward the end of the seventeenth century so many restrictions were enforced by the private investors who ruled the colony that the economy of the islands was being crippled. The colonists petitioned the Crown and sued the company, and the company forfeited its charter in 1684. The economy picked up. The Bermudians built ships of the fragrant cedar and traded in salt and food with the West Indies and America. Some became successful privateers during England's seemingly endless wars with France and Spain.

The Norwegian ship Gramma, first ship on St. George's slip

Bermuda's Seafarers and Their Sloops

This is how Sir Robert Robinson, who became Governor in 1687, described Bermuda in his day: "The people are of quick growth and well look't English countenance, but of a browner complexion, tall, lean, strong-limb'd and well-proportion'd. They are very frugal in their apparel, eating, drinking, and house furniture. Their houses are very neat and clean, usually of wood but an increasing number of stone."

He wrote that the men are "hardy and generally good sailors... The women are likewise of large growth and are skilful in swimming and pilotting. They are commonly good housewives and are very amorous. They are generally handsome and courtly, love their husbands, their children and their dress. The children are chiefly exercised in fishing, swimming, diving and digging, and not in education which their parents do not covet nor does the island easily afford." There were said to be three women to one man on the islands, since so many men lost their lives in shipwrecks.

It is easy to see why from the beginning Bermudians won wide fame as seafarers and boatbuilders. They had the deep, blue ocean all round them, their English heritage — and the great red cedar. Bermuda sloops came to be acclaimed as the best in the world for swiftness and long life. Bermuda was sacked by pirates more than thirty times in the seventeenth and eighteenth centuries, but it is more than probable that Bermudians gained more through their privateering than they lost to pirates.

During the seventeenth century, Bermuda onions became a considerable item in export. In 1719, straw hats made of plaited Bermuda palmetto came into vogue among London ladies, and the palmetto "straw" was important in the export trade for some time. The soft limestone of the islands was cut into blocks, used as ballast, and traded as a building material in the West Indies and the Bahamas. It came into use as a versatile building material on the islands. It can be cut with a handsaw when it is first dug, and hardens when exposed to air. Blocks of the stone were used to make walls of buildings, and thin tiles were cut from it to roof the houses. The tiles are very porous when first cut, but when white-washed with lime and exposed to the air for some time they cannot be penetrated by water.

The Koo-I-Noor, handsomest of Bermuda's clipper barques, launched 1855

The Eighteenth Century

The eighteenth century opened with years of great hardship and a series of governors with whom the people feuded and bickered. Governor Samuel Day was called a tyrant, and it was said he clipped the edges of the coins to enrich himself. Governor Henry Pullein was a privateer and a rogue. Governor John Hope was, on the other hand, gallant and admired by the Bermudians.

Bermuda and the American Revolution

The news of the shots fired at Bunker Hill was received, when it finally reached Bermuda on its way around the world, with consternation. The majority of the islanders were Loyalists, though a number of prominent families sympathized with the American colonists. War between England and her American colonies meant that Bermuda's food supply would be cut off and trade would be ruined.

The American colonists desperately needed gunpowder, while Bermudians sent delegates to the Continental Congress in Philadelphia in 1775 to beg for food. General George Washington promptly wrote to the inhabitants of the islands, asking for their sympathy. He said that he was informed that there was a very large powder magazine on Bermuda with a feeble guard, and asked tactfully if the American colonists might avail themselves of this supply. On a dark night in 1775 a band of quiet and speedy men broke into the powder magazine on Bermuda and rolled one hundred barrels of gunpowder down the hill through the back park of the staunchly Loyalist governor. They were loaded into whale-boats waiting along the shore and taken to sloops ready to sail. Rewards were posted for information leading to the conviction of the culprits, but they were never apprehended.

As a result, the Continental Congress authorized the shipment of a year's provisions to Bermuda. Bermudians also sailed from Turk's Island with salt for the Americans, who needed that commodity. As the war went on, the famished islanders on Bermuda became more and more dependent on American corn. Britain then sent victuals.

Continued on page 54

Approaching Bermuda
————*From East*

————*From West*

Hamilton, View from Paget

For detailed description of pictures see pages 49 to 53

Fort Hamilton

Hamilton Harbour

On Busy Front Street, Hamilton

Remembrance Ceremony at Cenotaph, Hamilton

For detailed description of pictures see pages 49 to 53

House of Assembly

Perot Post Office
and Public Library,
Hamilton

Par-La-Ville Gardens

The Government House
(Pembroke)

The Bermuda Cathedral (Anglican)

The City Hall of Hamilton

St. Theresa's R.C. Church, Hamilton

Paget on Hamilton Harbour

For detailed description of pictures see pages 49 to 53

Salt Kettle (Paget)

The Princess Hotel, Hamilton

Belmont Golf Course (Warwick)

Elbow Beach Hotel (Paget)

Into the Sunset

Jobson Cove (Warwick)

Horseshoe Bay (Southampton)

The Passion Flower

Bermudiana

FLOWERS OF BERMUDA

Cat's Claw- Vine

Mesembryanthemum

Botanical Gardens (Paget)

The Old Christ Church (Warwick)

Native Building Material

Southampton Princess

Sonesta Beach Hotel

Teddy Tucker, Famous Treasure Diver,
with Part of his Treasure.

Teddy Tucker's Famous Gold and Emerald Cross

Diving in the Clear Waters of Bermuda

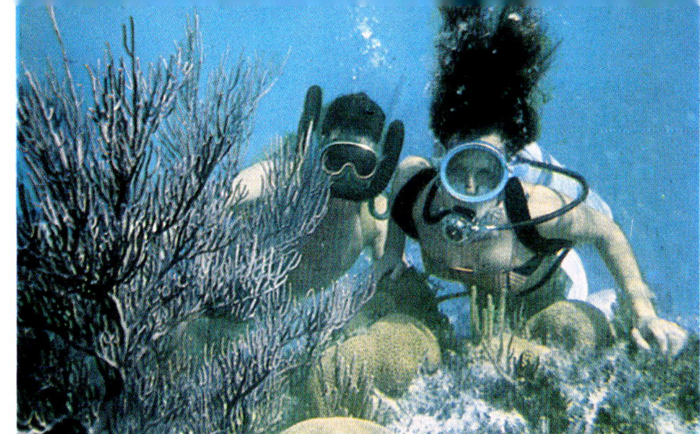

Ely's Harbour

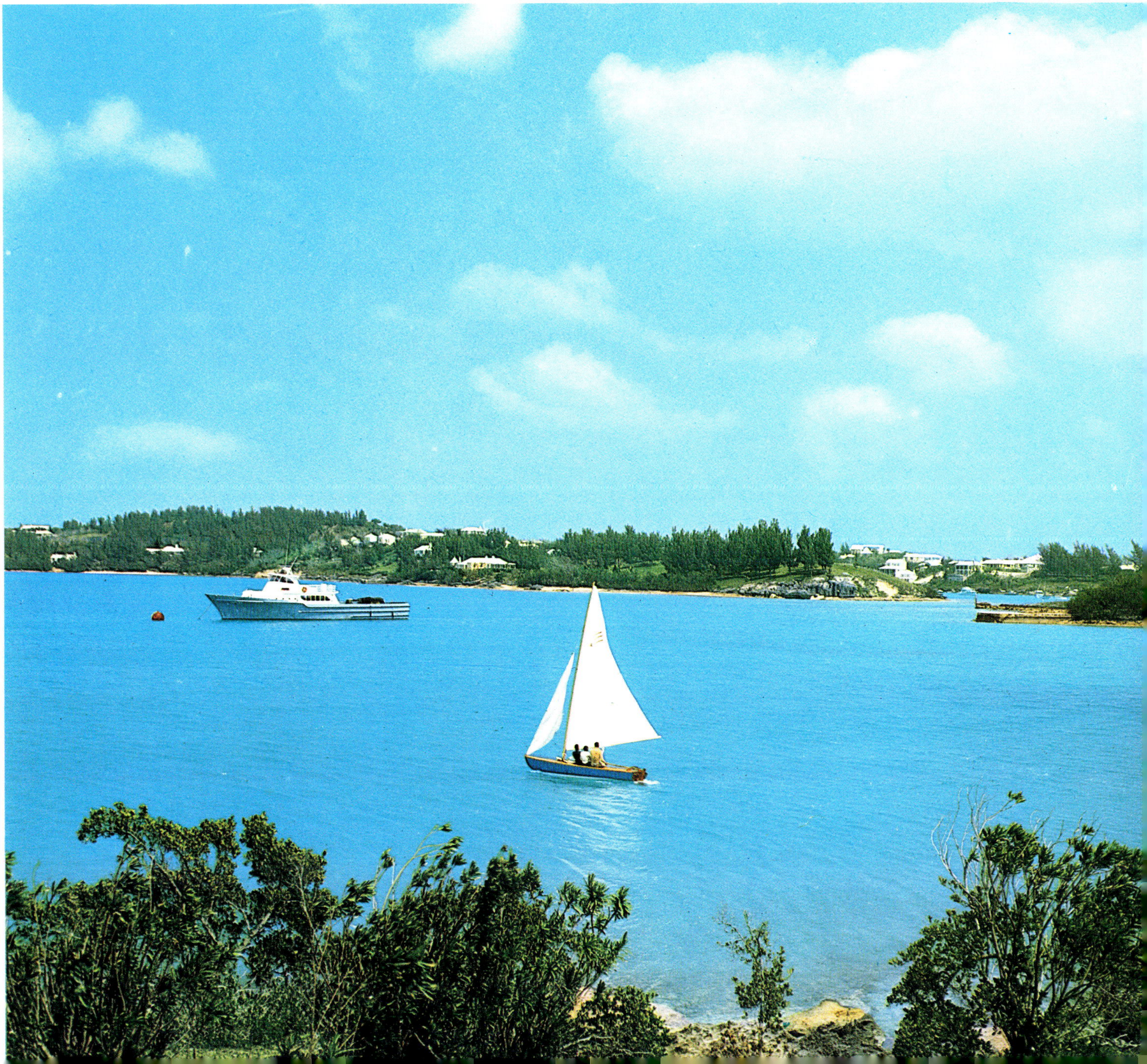

Paget with Salt Kettle.

A Sailboat Race

*Mangrove Bay
from Cambridge Beaches (Sandys)*

Mermaid Beach (Warwick)

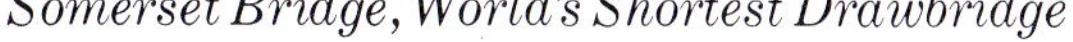

Riddell's Bay Golf and Country Club (Warwick)

For detailed description of pictures see pages 49 to 53

Somerset Bridge, World's Shortest Drawbridge

Cambridge Beaches (Sandys)

Gibb's Hill Lighthouse (Southampton)

Page 25

APPROACHING BERMUDA

The island group of Bermuda is clearly visible here from one end to the other, its picturesque shoreline broken by coves and sounds. The upper photograph shows the approach from the east in the late afternoon, with St. George's and St. David's Islands in the foreground. The second picture, taken from a lower angle, shows the beautiful colors of the clear ocean around Bermuda.

Page 26

HAMILTON, VIEW FROM PAGET

Hamilton is the capital of Bermuda. Located directly on Hamilton Harbour, it is a colorful and picturesque town with many interesting ancient buildings and sites and outstanding modern buildings. The city was founded in 1790 as the capital and was named after Henry Hamilton, the governor of Bermuda, who supported the proposal of many Bermudians to move the capital from St. George's on the east end of Bermuda to this central location.

Page 27

FORT HAMILTON

Overlooking the city of Hamilton and the harbour from the east, Fort Hamilton is one of the newer fortifications of Bermuda. Construction started on the fort in 1841 and was completed by 1889.

HAMILTON HARBOUR

This far extending safe harbour is a meeting place for elegant cruise ships of many countries. It is the heart of Hamilton, capital of Bermuda. Government buildings, banks, hotels and some of the most elegant stores are situated on Front Street, following the outline of the harbour.

Page 28

ON BUSY FRONT STREET, HAMILTON

Front Street, beside the Harbour of Hamilton, is one of the main streets of the capital city. The policeman who directs traffic on the busy corner of Queen and Front Streets is called "The Bobby in the Birdcage."

Page 29

REMEMBRANCE CEREMONY at CENOTAPH, HAMILTON

The Cenotaph is Bermuda's war memorial. Visible behind is a gray Georgian building, now called the Cabinet building, the meeting place for the Cabinet and the Senate, Bermuda's Upper House. It houses the offices of the Premier and the Cabinet.

HOUSE OF ASSEMBLY

Bermuda's House of Assembly, founded in 1620, is the second oldest representative institution in the Western World. Today it is the Lower House of Parliament and the meetings are held in the Sessions House in Hamilton.

Page 30

GOVERNMENT HOUSE (Pembroke)

Residence of the governors of Bermuda since 1892, Government House on top of Mt. Langton Hill has a commanding view of the city of Hamilton.

Page 31

PEROT POST OFFICE AND PUBLIC LIBRARY, HAMILTON

This is a view from Par-la-Ville Gardens in the back of two historical buildings. To the left is Par-la-Ville, on Queen Street, now the home of the Public Library and the Bermuda Historical Society Museum. To the right is Perot Post Office of philatelic fame. Here postmaster William B. Perot issued Bermuda's first postage stamps by writing his signature across the Hamilton postmark. Par-la-Ville was his home.

PAR-LA-VILLE GARDENS

A beautiful city garden in the heart of Hamilton between Queen Street and Par-la-Ville Road, it is a favorite meeting place, especially at the lunch hour. This photograph shows the fine collection of trees and flowers typical of Bermuda.

Page 32

THE BERMUDA CATHEDRAL (Anglican)

On top of Church Hill overlooking Hamilton stands the Bermuda Cathedral, an impressive building in Middle English-Gothic style. Nearby is the residence of the Lord Bishop of Bermuda.

THE CITY HALL OF HAMILTON

Modern, but fitting appropriately into the picture of Hamilton, the fine City Hall was completed in 1960. Its ninety-one-foot tower is a landmark of Hamilton. The building contains galleries of the Bermuda National Gallery and the Bermuda Society of Arts, and a theater. It is a civic center for the entire island group.

ST. THERESA'S CHURCH, THE ROMAN CATHOLIC CATHEDRAL

On Cedar Avenue, next door to Mount St. Agnes Academy, stands St. Theresa's Church, the Roman Catholic Cathedral, a modern building reminiscent of missions in California, a distinctive and fitting style for Bermuda.

Page 33

PAGET AND HAMILTON HARBOUR

Neighboring Pembroke Parish, in which the city of Hamilton is located, is the parish of Paget along the South Shore of Hamilton Harbour. The air view shows one of the idyllic residential sections along the harbour.

SALT KETTLE (Paget)

There is always lots of sailing, boating and other activities around Salt Kettle, a little peninsula with charming old homes and one of the liveliest little hotels, the Glencoe.

Page 34

THE PRINCESS HOTEL, HAMILTON

This beautiful modern hotel with its commanding location on Hamilton Harbour has a history, because it includes, in its present complex, parts of the old Princess Hotel, built in 1885. In the last decade of the nineteenth century, every celebrity coming to the island stayed or visited there.

ELBOW BEACH HOTEL (Paget)

One of the great hotels on the South Shore of Bermuda, is the Elbow Beach Hotel. Its big pool overlooks a magnificent private beach on the tranquil, leeward side of the island. The air view shows the stately hotel to the right, the beautiful gardens behind the beach and the tennis courts to the left. In the far background is the city of Hamilton.

Page 35

GOLF AT BELMONT (Warwick)

Bermuda is a paradise for golfers. Many of the great golf courses of the world are found here, and one of them is the Belmont, surrounding the Belmont Hotel and Golf Club. It is an eighteen-hole, par-68 course with beautiful views over the Great Sound.

Page 36

INTO THE SUNSET…JOBSON COVE (Warwick)

The South Shore of Bermuda has many romantic smaller and larger coves with idyllic sandy beaches. The lower picture shows such a cove, Jobson Cove in Warwick; the upper picture the mouth of such a cove at sunset.

Page 37

HORSESHOE BAY (Southampton)

The most beautiful public beach of Bermuda is undoubtedly at Horseshoe Bay. Stretching for about half a mile along the South Shore, it has the finest of white-sand beaches, framed by dramatic rock formations that shelter sun-bathers from the wind.

Page 38

BOTANICAL GARDENS

The Botanical Gardens are situated in eastern Paget and contain many interesting specimens. Admission is free and there are tours several times a week as well as a visitor's center. These are magnificent gardens with a wide variety of flowers.

Page 39

FLOWERS OF BERMUDA:

THE PASSION FLOWER

This exotic flower, grown commercially in Bermuda, is a favorite for corsages and flower arrangements. The vine on which it grows thrives in the islands.

BERMUDIANA

A native of the islands, this lovely blue flower blooms profusely from March to May, especially along the beaches. It is the national flower of Bermuda.

CAT'S-CLAW VINE

Typical of Bermuda is this yellow flower of the vine that grows on old walls all over the islands.

MESEMBRYANTHEMUM

This subtropical succulent plant with its trailing habit of growth blooms luxuriantly in Bermuda.

Page 40
THE OLD CHRIST CHURCH (Church of Scotland), WARWICK

This church, built in 1719, is the oldest Presbyterian church in the western hemisphere. Adjoining is Thorburn Memorial Hall, erected in memory of Reverend Walter Thorburn, minister of the church from 1852 to 1882.

NATIVE BUILDING MATERIAL

Carved into many hillsides in Bermuda are huge quarries from which big blocks of stone are cut by hand-saws. The soft limestone is later cut into building blocks. Initially it absorbs moisture, and it becomes hardened with exposure to the air.

Page 41
THE SOUTHAMPTON PRINCESS HOTEL

Dominating the heights of Southampton is the new Southampton Princess Hotel with an attractive 18-hole, par-3 golf course leading down to the beautiful private cove beach on the quiet South Shore of Bermuda.

SONESTA BEACH HOTEL

With its unusual location on a rock formation surrounded by a splendid beach of the South Shore of Southampton, the Sonesta Beach Hotel is one of the best hotels in Bermuda.

Page 42
TEDDY TUCKER WITH PART OF HIS TREASURE

Bermuda-born Teddy Tucker is an internationally famous treasure diver who has salvaged treasures worth millions of dollars from sunken ships in waters around Bermuda.

TEDDY TUCKER'S FAMOUS GOLD AND EMERALD CROSS

In an astonishing outrage this sixteenth-century gold and emerald cross was stolen just before it was to be shown to Queen Elizabeth II at the opening of the Bermuda Maritime Museum in 1975.

Page 43
ELY'S HARBOUR

Bermuda's most western bay is Ely's Harbour, a sheltered stretch of water that is perfect for small-craft sailing, water skiing, and other aquatic sports.

DIVING IN THE CLEAR WATERS OF BERMUDA

Bermuda is the most northern island group around which corals now grow. Brain coral, gorgonians, and softly waving sea-fans, surrounded by colorful fish, make a vivid impression on the reef diver. The picture shows gorgonians to the right and brain coral in the center.

Page 44

MANGROVE BAY FROM CAMBRIDGE BEACHES

At the northwest end of Bermuda on Sandys' coast is Mangrove Bay, with some of the most romantic scenery in the islands. The picture shows a view to the southeast over the Bay, with Somerset Village in the background.

Page 45

PAGET WITH SALT KETTLE

A bird's-eye view from Great Sound over Hinson Island to Paget shows the Inverurie Hotel to the right and Salt Kettle in the center. The picture was taken after an ocean race, and the yachts are resting in safe water.

A SAILBOAT RACE

Races are a favorite sport in Bermuda on weekends and on special occasions.

Page 46

MERMAID BEACH

Here is another romantic beach, surrounded by picturesque rock formations. It is part of a cottage colony of the same name on the South Shore of Warwick.

Page 47

RIDDELL'S BAY GOLF AND COUNTRY CLUB (Warwick)

On the eastern shore of Little Sound on the west end of Warwick is Bermuda's oldest golf club surrounding Riddell's Bay. It was designed in 1922 by Devereux Emmett.

SOMERSET BRIDGE, WORLD'S SHORTEST DRAWBRIDGE

Said to be the shortest drawbridge in the world, Somerset Bridge connects Southampton with Somerset Island in Sandys Parish.

Page 48

CAMBRIDGE BEACHES (Sandys)

On the northern end of Sandys Parish are the Cambridge Beaches, a peninsula with beautiful beaches and good hotel accommodations.

GIBB'S HILL LIGHTHOUSE, SOUTHAMPTON

Situated 239 feet above sea level, the lighthouse overlooks the northwestern approach to Hamilton from the Great Sound. It is one of the most powerful lights of the world's shipping lanes and has been in operation since May 1, 1846.

Continued from Page 24

In the end, Bermuda largely remained loyal to the Crown. Bermuda privateers raided American shipping, and Bermuda's ships were captured and invasion was threatened by the American revolutionaries. Many Loyalists from the thirteen American colonies came to the islands.

Nowhere was peace more welcome than on Bermuda. Trading resumed and times got better. The **Bermuda Gazette,** the first newspaper, was started in 1784.

HAMILTON

Smith's Island was the first seat of government. Soon the government was moved to St. George's Towne. As a capital, St. George's Towne, on the eastern end of the island chain, was not ideally situated. A central location would be much more convenient. Governors began to try to change the capital to a more central location early in the eighteenth century. The problem was, as one writer noted in that era, "for the last forty years each individual has been aiming at a Towne within a hundred yards of his nativity."

Construction of the Town of Hamilton began in 1792 with the backing of Governor Henry Hamilton, after whom it is named. The capital was moved in 1815 during Admiral Cockburn's administration.

A custom house warehouse was built, and four forts to defend the islands against the French. A coffee house and stores soon followed. Merchants began to grow wealthy through their ownership of shares in privateering vessels operating in the West Indies. A visiting acrobat performed in Hamilton in 1796. As the years went swiftly by, schools and churches were built, fire and fever occasionally hit, and the sea which dominates Bermuda shaped the life of the delightful town rising on the rolling hills above the harbor. Hamilton has never been a dull town, having always been prone to balls, quadrilles, band concerts, and flirtations.

Hamilton Harbour, circa 1868

Tom Moore in Bermuda

Tom Moore the Irish poet, strolled the streets and lanes of Bermuda but briefly, but the memory of his curls and charm and of his lyrics is still fresh in the islands, and his was Bermuda's most celebrated flirtation. He was what all Irishmen want to be — handsome, a poet, and a great social success. He came young out of Ireland to London, floating on the crest of the popularity of his first lyrics. His social success in London proved so expensive that he was glad, with the help of a princely patron, to go to Bermuda in 1803 as registrar of the admiralty prize courts in the islands.

He did not make the money he had been led to believe would be his, and so he stayed only three months. But while there he flirted, was wined and dined, and stored memories that led him to write most fondly of those islands and of a lady who lived there. His charm caused him to be most hospitably received, and it is of this hospitality, in part, that he later sang. To a young matron seven months married, he wrote the verses of "Nea."

That she was indeed a Bermudian, the scenery of the verse attests:

"Behold the leafy mangrove, bending
  O'er the waters blue and bright,
Like Nea's silky lashes, lending
  Shadow to her eyes of light!"

His "Ode to the Calabash Tree" is still so well remembered that "Moore's calabash tree," under which he sat, is pointed out today, dense and luxuriant with age. The golden sands, the tint of bowers, the cottages "white as the palace of a Lapland gnome" — Moore wrote about them all. The flavor, the fragrance, and the beauty of Bermuda were recalled by Tom Moore long after his three months' stay in the islands. Nine years later he wrote:

"Oh, had we some bright little isle of our
                                        own,
In a blue summer ocean far off and alone...
Where simply to feel that we breathe,
                                  that we live
Is worth the best joy that life elsewhere
                                   can give."

He was not the first nor the last to feel the magic of Bermuda, but he captured it so deftly in his lyrics that he is still well enshrined in island legends.

Moore appointed a deputy in Bermuda and returned to London, where he wrote successful poems, lyrics for songs, satires, and political squibs. The deputy he left in Bermuda embezzled a large sum, for which Moore was liable, and Moore had to go live on the Continent to avoid debtors' prison until he negotiated a settlement of the Bermuda affair. This does not seem to have soured his memories of the islands.

THE NAPOLEONIC WARS

After a brief period of brisk trade between Bermuda and the rest of the world following the end of the American Revolution, war between England and France heated up. If there had been mixed emotions in Bermuda regarding the American Revolution, there were none in the Napoleonic Wars or in the War of 1812-1815 between England and the United States. Bermudians were totally loyal to England. French privateers raided Bermuda shipping, and Bermuda privateers excelled all others. Admiral Nelson, who had served in the West Indies, finally sank Napoleon's dream by sending the French fleet to the bottom at the Battle of Trafalgar Bay in 1805, where Nelson won immortality and lost his life. For the fastest way to get the news of the victory and the loss to England, the English sent it in a Bermuda sloop, the **Pickle.**

It was from Bermuda, through the North Rock passage, that the British fleet took off in 1814 to attack the capital of the United States. With 3,500 troops aboard and a good passage to the Chesapeake, this fleet attacked and burned Washington.

THE DOCKYARD

It became so obvious that Bermuda might become the Gibraltar of the West if properly fortified that in 1810 Britain began to build a dockyard and a naval station on Ireland Island. Work began with local labor and British funds. The movement to build a mighty fortress there began in the American Revolution and resulted finally in Bermuda's becoming the headquarters of the America and West Indies Squadron of the Royal Navy. To assist in the work on the dockyard, convicts were sent out from England for forty years. More than 9,000 men were sent to Bermuda from England in that period, and old ships were used for their prisons. They not only worked on the dockyard, they cut roads into the limestone. The Imperial Dockyard on the West End was a tremendous boon to the islands' economy in the nineteenth century, and not until 1951 was it closed.

The Bermuda Clippers

The first steamship came into Hamilton Harbour in 1833, amazing those seafaring islanders. But the greatest days of the sailing ships were yet to come. Those great white birds of the nineteenth century, that could move across the water faster than the early steamships, became known as Yankee clippers. They originated, however, in Baltimore, where the first big clipper was built in 1833. The Bermuda shipbuilders contributed their share to the beauty that followed, spurred by the competition of the new steamships.

Some of the fastest and most graceful ships that ever sailed were the clipper barques built on Bermuda during the 1850s and 1860s. They were long, slender vessels with a long, sharp, bow. They carried three rakish masts, and the square-rigged sails were crowded on. Veteran seamen said at the time they were launched that they were the most beautiful things ever built in Bermuda. They sailed for decades between Bermuda and New York, the West Indies and Britain. They beat steamships. The five fast Bermuda clippers built in Bermuda between 1853 and 1864 were the **Sir George F. Seymour,** the **Koh-I-Noor,** the **Pearl,** the **Cedric** and the **Lady Milne.**

The clippers carried arrowroot, onions, potatoes, tomatoes, passengers, and convicts going home to Ireland from Bermuda, and they returned with supplies to the island. Arrowroot, from which a fine starch is made, was a staple of the island trade at that time. Whales were still taken along the coast, furnishing not only oil but "sea beef." When William Reid came out in 1839 to serve as governor, he found only two ploughs in Bermuda. He imported more ploughs and held ploughing contests, and the export of arrowroot increased. The first lighthouse was built during his term as governor, and the whale-oil light went on in 1846 on Gibb's Hill. He also founded a public library in 1839, the first on Bermuda.

Floating Dock, 1885

The Civil War in the United States

To Bermuda, as to the Bahamas, the Civil War in the United States from 1861 to 1865 brought a great tide of prosperity. The sympathy of the majority of Bermudians was with the South, for many had families or trade relations in Virginia, North Carolina, and South Carolina. Since Bermuda men excelled on the sea, they proved to be great blockade runners. England, with mills that needed cotton, shipped arms, ammunition, and other badly needed supplies to the South through Bermuda. It was a rewarding if highly dangerous test of skill in the fast, shallow-draft Bermuda sloops to evade the Northern ships blockading Southern ports. St. George's and Hamilton Harbour were thronged with ships, and their warehouses and wharves were crammed with goods going and coming.

Though Queen Victoria had forbidden her subjects to get involved in that war, few doubted the South would win, and the blockade-runners were heroes in Bermuda. Many ships were seized or sunk. Many more made fortunes. The United States Navy attempted to blockade St. George's Harbour but desisted after sharp protests by British authorities.

An economic slump followed the American Civil War, and the building up of Bermuda as a major British fortress of the Atlantic again helped to save the colony from an economic downturn.

Trouble threatened with Venezuela. Victorian land forces were stationed in Bermuda, and barracks were built for them near the naval forts at the dockyard. Nine large forts were repaired or built. The largest floating dock, the most modern facility to serve ships of its time, was towed across the Atlantic to Bermuda in 1869. The thirty-six-day trip was an uneventful success, to the delight and wonder of the islanders.

THE PORTUGUESE

To take up the slack in the economy after the Civil War, the Bermudians also concentrated on agriculture and on increasing their exports. The population concentrated on growing potatoes, onions, and tomatoes for export in the chilly season when vegetables could not be grown in North America. With the increase in vegetable farming and export, Portuguese farmers came in from the Azores. They were the migrant workers of their day. They were welcomed, and many stayed to live in Bermuda. More Portuguese were brought in from the Azores in 1923-1924, when the same farm labor was needed. Today there are several thousand Bermudians of Portuguese descent, characterized by thrift and energy.

*A blockade runner at anchor in St. George's Harbour during the
American Civil War. This 1860s picture is owned by the Bermuda
National Trust and was painted by an English artist, Edward James.
    Also at anchor are sailing ships, which carried cargoes from
Europe to be loaded on the small, fast steamers to run President
Lincoln's naval blockade. The cargoes varied from arms and medicines
to hoop skirts and French perfumes.*

Seeds of the Tourist Industry

Before there was a United States of America, Bermuda had achieved a reputation as a delightful place to visit because of its healthful climate. In 1779 Maryland showed her goodwill to the many islanders who were helping the American Revolutionaries by granting to one of her prominent citizens the right to go past the wartime embargo to visit Bermuda for his health. It was widely known even then for its fine climate for invalids.

With the renewed endeavor to raise and export vegetables to the United States and Canada during the last half of the nineteenth century, the ships that carried the freight away from the islands began also to carry passengers. They were not the modern, luxurious cruise ships of today. Mark Twain said, "Bermuda is a paradise ... but one must go through hell to get there." William Dean Howells, Mark Twain's friend, wrote in 1885 of Bermuda's capital, Hamilton, "I should think it a rich enough experience to spend my whole time lounging up and down the sloping streets." Princess Louise, daughter of Queen Victoria and wife of the governor general of Canada, visited Bermuda in 1882. The princess conquered hearts and was conquered by the charms of the islands. She drove about in a little phaeton and sailed about in a skiff.

Promptly, a second hotel called The Princess was built in Hamilton in her honor. A new bank was founded. Three large schools which still serve Bermuda were founded between 1888 and 1893, Saltus Grammar School, Mount St. Agnes Academy, and Bermuda High School for Girls. Tourists began to come in sufficient numbers to keep two hotels open all year, and before long there were other hotels open only in the winter.

The reputation of Bermuda grew, and more and more visitors came to relax, get warm in the winter, and restore their souls with beauty. The island became one of the first winter resorts for North America and probably inspired Henry Flagler's Palm Beach. A new lighthouse, St. David's Lighthouse, began to shine in 1879. A regatta had been organized for Princess Louise, and in 1882 the first organized Bermuda dinghy races were sailed. Tennis was introduced into Bermuda from England in 1873, and from Bermuda into the United States. Telephones were introduced in 1887 and electric light in 1904. Sir Thomas Lipton put up a cup for the first of the Biennial Ocean Races, which was sailed in 1906. The islands had always been hospitable, from the time the shipwrecked English colonists headed for Jamestown came ashore in 1609. It dawned upon the Bermudians that hospitality to visitors could be an attractive industry and a pleasant way of life. Tourism, that great industry of the twentieth century, was born.

Mark Twain in Bermuda, circa 1907

WORLD WAR I

War in 1914 again meant hardship to Bermuda, with shipping crippled and supplies limited. Bermuda fishermen could not go to the outermost banks for fear of being captured by German warships. Bermuda volunteers and militia were mobilized to guard the island fortress of the British Navy. Bermuda contingents served with the British Army in France.

PROHIBITION

No single event had such a stimulating and immediate effect on Bermuda's economic well-being as the passage of the Volstead Act in the United States. Tourists flocked in to drink decent whiskey in a uniquely beautiful little island resort. Luxury liners plied the sea between Bermuda and New York and kept the new hotels that were being built full of visitors. The Mid-Ocean Golf Course was created. Bermuda seafarers turned their talents to rum-running. The islands boomed.

The Suntan Revolution

In the 1920s a profound cultural change began to come about in the United States, and later it spread to some extent in England. It was to have a wide effect that still continues. Bermuda pioneered in contributing to the change. This change was in the attitude of well-to-do people toward being suntanned. For ages a fair complexion had been considered most elegant and desirable among people of English origin. The skin tones of blond ladies unkissed by the sun were what English poets praised. In the United States, and especially in the South, a "peaches - and - cream" complexion was prized as proof of the fact that the possessor thereof did not have to work in the fields

The Princess Hotel, 1885

in the sun. Sun bonnets had excellent sales. Then the rich and famous began in considerable numbers to go vacationing in Bermuda — sailing, golfing, swimming. A suntan began to have prestige. It was proof positive in winter that anyone who sported a browned skin could afford to take the time off and to spend the money needed to go to sunny lands to play.

After a suntan became a status symbol, Bermuda's summer tourism received a big boost. The climate had always been pleasant in the summer, and the water more inviting for water sports than in the winter. A year-round tourist economy was born, and it continued to prosper in the 1930s even during Depression in the United States.

In spite of this profound sociological change, Bermuda did not give women the right to vote until 1944. It was not until the 1950s that South Florida resorts were able to achieve the stability that results from attracting summer sun-lovers in considerable numbers.

WORLD WAR II

The tourist economy went into hibernation in this war, but the economic effects were not so brutal as in other countries. German submarines became so menacing to North Atlantic shipping that Great Britain asked Bermuda to give land for the establishment of U.S. naval and military bases. One-tenth of the land of the islands was given on a ninety-nine-year lease, and shoal waters were also filled to build the bases. These became vital to the safety of the convoys of men and material that helped to defeat Hitler. From these islands the Royal Navy patrolled the Atlantic. The United States built an airfield that still serves Bermuda today.

THE SPACE RACE

The peacetime alliance between Bermuda and the United States was strengthened when in 1959 the U.S. National Aeronautics and Space Administration was given the right to build a tracking station for space vehicles on Cooper's Island. Bermuda has also been a major base for the exploration of "inner space", the ocean. In 1964, Operation Sealab was carried out thirty miles southwest of Bermuda on the Argus Bank. This scientific experiment tested the ability of men to live deep underwater for ten days, and was followed by many other experiments.

Privateers and Pirates of Bermuda

Piracy and privateering began to flourish in the West Indies early in the sixteenth century. Attacks on the Spanish treasure fleets by bold spirits, first from France and then from Holland, began as early as the 1520s. The English soon joined them. Some of these pirate-privateers were highly respected, such as Sir John Hawkins and Sir Francis Drake. Sir Francis Drake declared that "an act of piracy against that cursed papist [The King of Spain] is an act of piety, so help us God." And Queen Elizabeth II addressed Sir Francis, scourge of the Spanish, as "my dear pyrate." Small tenant farmers and younger sons, as well as noble adventurers, were attracter to free-booting.

About the time Bermuda was being founded, piracy was flourishing not only in the Caribbean, but also in the North Sea, the English Channel, and the Mediterranean. Idleness was the background of much piracy, it is reported, and Ireland was the home of many pirates. Spain realized the importance of Bermuda as a bastion for pirates as soon as news reached Spain of colonizing by the English, but the small Spanish expedition sent against the young colony in 1614 backed off when fired upon.

Bermuda seafarers were turning to piracy, "because their fingers itched," within two decades of the founding of the colony. Bermuda officials also, early in the islands' history, were doing business with pirates. Ships commissioned in England to take pirates became pirates, which was the story of Sir Henry Morgan. During the seventeenth century it was still considered patriotic for Englishmen to attack and capture Spanish ships on the high seas.

Bermudians, who so often lacked supplies, welcomed any tramp ship of the sea that was not unfriendly. In the early years of the islands' history the company controlling the islands actually feared that revolt to the pirates by the people would take place, because of company mismanagement. By the middle of the seventeenth century, English and Dutch pirates infested Bermuda waters. Because the interests of the company were not identical with those of the colonists, and because the colonists were crippled by trade restrictions and administrative policies, the Bermudians were not reluctant to deal with pirates who did not harm them, and many of the islands' officials were rather openly corrupt.

The real license for respectable piracy by British seamen came in the eighteenth century and began with the War of Jenkins' Ear in 1739. Respectable sea banditry was called privateering. For almost a century after that time, privateering was big business in Bermuda. The period began with a treaty between England and Spain whereby England had the privilege of sending supplies in one ship each year either to Cartagena or Portobello in the Spanish West Indies. English merchants, being what they were in that era, began to send two ships, sometimes to both cities. One ship would land and discharge her cargo. At night, the ship would again be loaded with supplies from the second merchantman, standing offshore out of sight. The Spanish frequently showed their resentment at the violation of the treaty by attacking the illegal number two ship. One that they so attacked belonged to a sea captain called Jenkins, and he said the Spanish took not only his ship but his ear.

Jenkins showed his pickled ear round London and elicited such sympathetic rage that the populace wanted war. English officialdom said that Jenkins lost his ear for one of those crimes that had sent him to English prisons several times. The people prevailed, and England went to war against Spain. For about seventy-five years thereafter, England continued a series of almost unbroken wars with her European neighbors and, finally, toward the end of the period, with her American colonies.

Wealthy merchantmen of Bermuda promptly responded to the situation by fitting out privateers. The privateer captain had to have letters of marque to authorize him to attack enemy ships. There were a number of regulations governing the business, including the requirement that the privateer owner bring back his prize ship to an admiralty court, so that the court could make a judgment as to the legality of its seizure and as to the awards, based upon the value of the ship's cargo. Some of the swiftest ships ever built in Bermuda went to sea as privateers.

This is the way a privateersman was described in the eighteenth century: "Your true privateersman is a sort of half-horse, half-alligator, with a streak of lightening in his composition — something like a man-of-war's man, but much more like a pirate, with a superabundance of whisker, as if he held with Samson that his strength was in the quantity of his hair." Privateersmen, it is reported, were nowhere well-disciplined and on shore were frequently disorderly.

Commissioning privateers who raided enemy shipping for profit obviously made good sense to England; they were the guerilla troops of the ocean. But they finagled around, evaded regulations as to disposal of their cargoes, carried two sets of papers, and flouted the laws regulating privateering in all sorts of ways, including bribery of admiralty courts in Bermuda. They were not supposed to broach their cargo before it was adjudicated by an admiralty court, but this was a common practice. Many a privateersman was accused of attacking friendly shipping under false colors. The business thrived in the American Revolution and in the Napoleonic Wars, when French shipping was the enemy. The stakes were high — death or wealth. But there was no risk of life or limb to the Bermuda merchants who backed these seafaring ventures and reaped fortunes.

The lawless era came to an end in 1815, when peace treaties were made between England and the United States. While it lasted, it was a rough, jolly time.

APPEARANCE AND ORIGIN

Mention of Bermuda to those who know the islands evokes the image of curving pink-sand beaches backed by shell-gray rocks, gently rolling hills, and dunes — all surrounded by a turquoise sea. The coloring is that of El Greco. Bermuda is a tiny citadel of beauty alone in the vast Atlantic. The nearest land is Cape Hatteras, 568 miles due west, in North Carolina. Bermuda is 2,950 miles from Liverpool, England. Because the first mariners were so surprised to find this lonely speck of land in the ocean, without any apparent reason for its being, Bermuda emerges into history clouded with myth.

There are seven chief islands and about 131 smaller ones large enough to have been

A view of St. George's, 1816

named. The group is attenuated, it arcs into a fish-hook, and the seven principal islands are linked by bridges. They are, from east to west, St. George's, St. David's, the Main Island, Somerset, Watford, Boaz, and Ireland. The total area is 20.59 square miles. The chain of islands is fifteen miles long and two and a half miles wide at its greatest width.

One of the fascinating things about Bermuda is that it is unique in appearance, flavor, and geography. If you had ever been there and were transported back by magic or a dream, you would immediately recognize that you were on Bermuda and nowhere else, even though you might have no landmarks or man-made structures to guide you in recognition. Palm trees flourish in the frost-free air, but this is not one of the tropical clusters of islands in the West Indies. Underlying the land is an old, extinct volcano, but there are no volcanic peaks rising into rain forests in the clouds. It is a rolling land, fertile in the valleys and on the lower slopes. The word that applies to the landscape of Bermuda is "gentle."

This is not true of the skyscape, which derives from the land. The clouds that float above the little specks of land are formed by them, and these towering cumulus shapes and feathery cirrus that ride the winds above them can only be called "noble." There are no sunsets more beautiful than those of Bermuda.

The sea may be as blue in some other favored spots, but nowhere is it bluer than in Bermuda. The seascapes give Bermuda its strength. All that marvelous blue Atlantic, unbroken all the way to the Canary Islands, comes surging in against the reefs and boulders that guard the pink-sand beaches — and the sea does not wear the islands down, it builds them up, on the whole.

Another thing that fascinates one about these islands is that, though they are so small, they give the effect of diversity. They have individual personalities. They can be explored with never-failing delight. This is because of the curving hills, the looping, intertwining shoreline, and the caves.

In its geological origin, Bermuda is not unique. The islands and the banks that lie round them are volcanic in origin and have other counterparts in the Atlantic and the Pacific. They are the peak of a volcanic ridge that began to rise from the floor of the ocean a hundred million years ago. In this they resemble the Lesser Antilles, Iceland, and the Azores. However, they have a limestone cap, and in this respect they are similar to the Bahamas.

When the cone of the volcano that was to become Bermuda reached above the ocean, it began to be eroded by waves and rain. Around the cone, just beneath the surface, a platform of eroded volcanic sand was formed. On the platform grew coral caps, and in the sand and along the beaches there were many molluscs. Shells became limestone sand, and the stone rose above the volcanic sands. In time, a thick cap of limestone and limey sandstone covered the old volcanic cone. The volcanic rock that is the base of the islands lies far beneath the sea's surface. Today Bermuda is on the northern margin of the Atlantic area in which coral grows, but in many eras in the past, when the seas were warmer, the coral colonies that extract

The Square of St. George's, Bermuda, 1823

lime from the sea and build the hard coral rock proliferated.

Much of Bermuda's surface rock is what is called aeolian limestone. This is formed when the wind piles limey sand into dunes and the rain cements the sand and lime into rock. What resulted in Bermuda is unusual. The sand piled into dunes by the wind and called calciferous sand is made from the particles of shell and old coral rock. This material tends to dissolve in the heavy rains. During the ice ages the water seeping into the sand carried sufficient calcium to cement the dunes into a rock that is named **aeolianite.** This is the stone that is so widely used as a building material.

Again and again during the ages, when the glaciers melted and reformed and the ocean rose and fell, this limestone-forming process went on. When the islands were above the sea, the rocks would weather, plants would grow, and soil would form. Geologists find in Bermuda a beautiful record of what went on in shore formations in the Ice Ages.

In Bermuda, bays and sounds curve in and around and between the islands and the rocks. Long lines of hills curve around ponds and marshes. There are no rivers or streams, nor is there any evidence that there ever have been. The lowlands are the result of the development of sinkholes between ridges. This kind of topography is called Karst, for the Karst region of Yugoslavia consists of limestone in which basins and caves have been scoured out. Because of the heavy rainfall, the summits of the hills have had the soil washed away, and they are usually rather bare of vegetation.

The surface stone is so porous that water flows through it under the island from the sea while rain water seeps down through the rock and floats on the salt. The fresh water layer is thickest in the middle of the island and is called the lens. The existence of this supply of water, available through vertical wells, was only discovered since the Second World War—in part thanks to a man with a dowsing rod, Henry Gross, who was brought to the island by the author Kenneth Roberts. Before that an ingenious system of providing the Hamilton area with water was developed by the entrepreneur, Sir Harry Watlington, who drew the water from the top of the Devonshire Marsh through horizontal wells. Water obtained by this system and then treated still serves the Hamilton area and several parishes.

The limestone of Bermuda is a rigid sponge. Where plants grow and die, humus is formed. When rain falls on this humus as it decays, humic acid is formed. When the acid percolates into limestone rocks, it dissolves some of the lime. This is the way in which the topographical features of Bermuda were formed. In most limey regions of the world where the process has gone on, streams, rivers, and lakes have been brought into being. But in Bermuda, because the islands are so very narrow and porous, there is no fresh water on the surface, but valleys, sinkholes, and caves have been shaped by the percolation of the rain. The eroded valleys and the bottoms of the sinkholes have rapidly become filled with alluvial soil, sand, and humus, and this soil is fertile.

One of the most memorable aspects of Bermuda is its pink sand. It does not take

Continued on page 103

St. George's Town

*The Ancient State House
St. George's*

St. David's Island

For detailed description of pictures see pages 97 to 102.

In St. George's Harbour

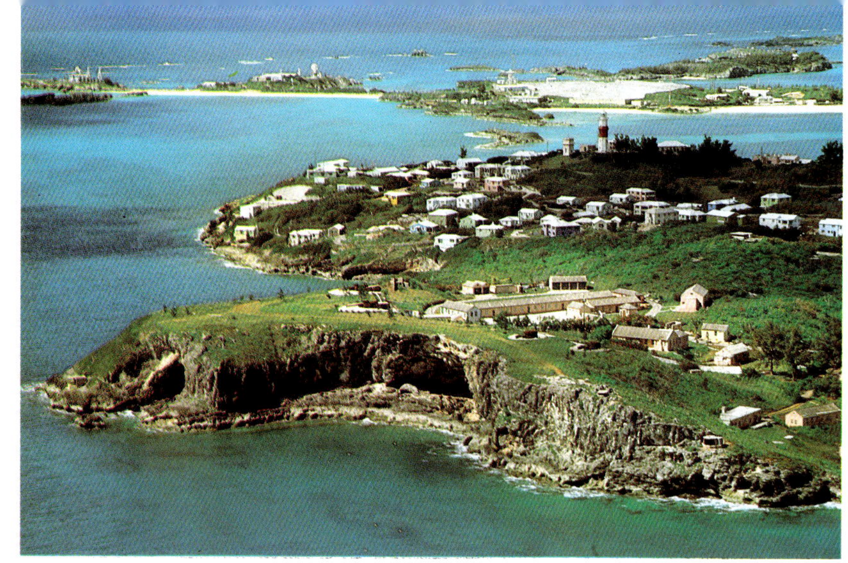

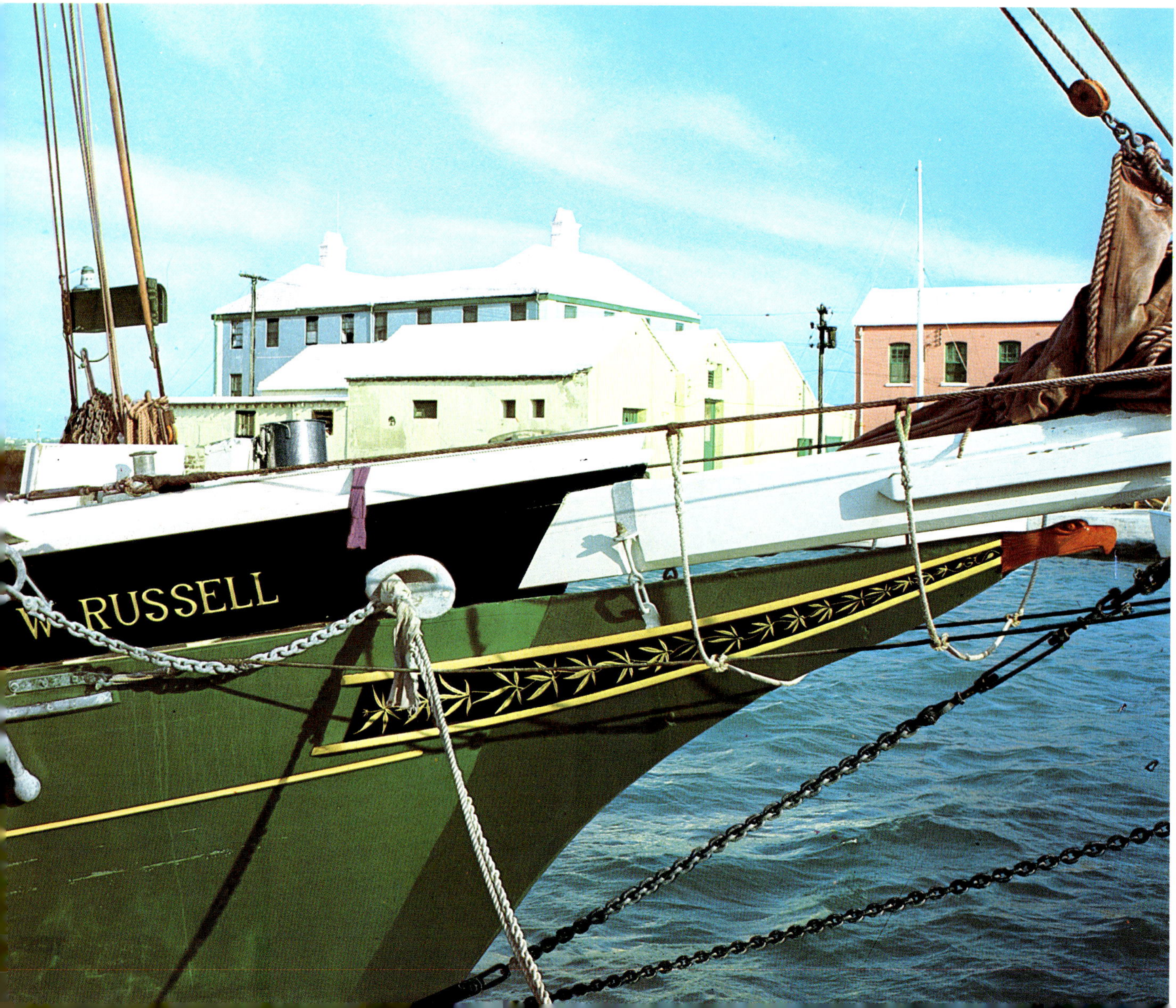

St. Peter's Church, St. George's

Old Graves at St. Peter's

Replica of the Deliverance

Fort St. Catherine

*On Shelly Bay
(Hamilton Parish)*

*Bermuda Aquarium
at Flatts Inlet*

*The Annual
Peppercorn Ceremo
St. George's*

Speaker of the House of Assembly

Noonday Cannon Salute, St. George's

BERMUDA
PAGEANTRY

*Skirling Ceremony
at Fort Hamilton*

The Bermuda Regiment at Gate's Fort

Opening of Parliament

The Old Rectory, St. George's

→

Typical Bermuda Roof, St. George's

Upper left: Tucker House
Left: Confederate Museum
Upper right: Joseph Stockdale House

HISTORICAL HOUSES IN ST. GEORGE'S

Historical Society Museum

St. George's Town Hall

The Old Bridge House

Church Ruins, St. George's

Fishing is Good in Bermuda

Tucker's Town Bay

Natural Arches,
Tucker's Town

Marriott's Castle Harbour Hotel,
Tucker's Town

Castle Island Beach

Castle Harbour Golf Club (First Hole)

Crystal Caves

NIGHT LIFE IN BERMUDA

Gene Steede, Noted Calypso Singer

Evening in Hamilton Harbour

The Royal Naval Dockyard

.___ Mid Ocean Golf Club,↑
Tucker's Town

Easter Lilies at the
Bermuda Perfumery

Palm Grove Garden (Devonshire)

North Coast at the Crawl

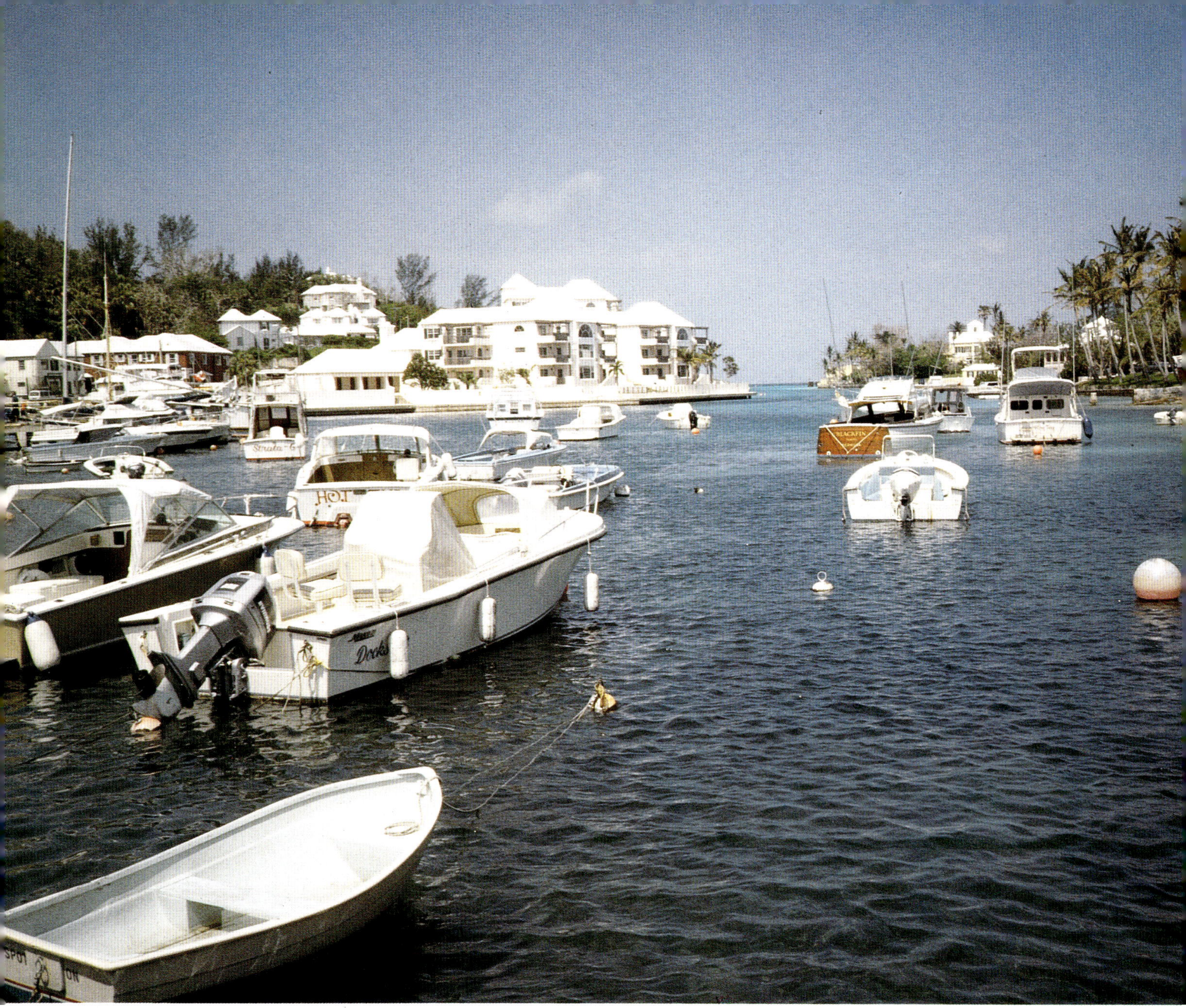

Flatts Inlet

Rental Transportation

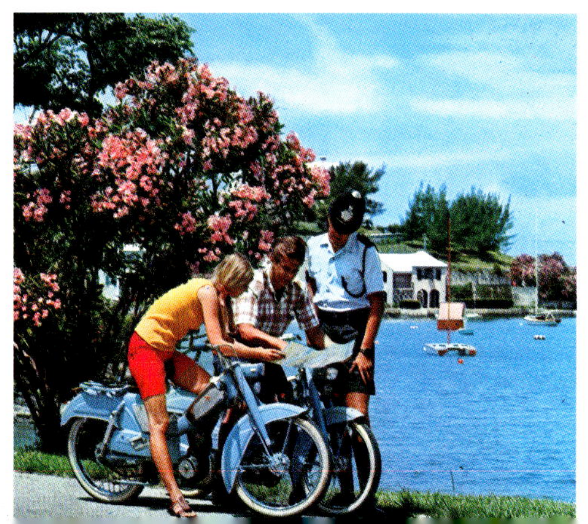

*South Shore at Tucker's Town with
Golf Courses and Castle Harbour Beach*

For detailed description of pictures see pages 97 to 102.

Tom Moore's Tavern

Page 73

ST. GEORGE'S TOWN

This view over the old town and harbour from the east shows its strategic location on the eastern entrance to the island. The small Ordnance Island in the middle of the harbour connected with the town by a bridge is clearly visible.

THE STATE HOUSE (St. George's)

Begun in 1620, built with irregular blocks of limestone, finished within three years, it is Bermuda's oldest building. It served until 1815 for the meetings of the General Assembly and as Court House.

Page 74

ST. DAVID'S ISLAND

At east end of Bermuda across the harbor of St. George's is St. David's Island. Its rocky shores and interesting history are described in some mystery novels. Its inhabitants are a mixture of mostly white, Negro and American Indians from the general population of Bermuda in the 19th century. In the 17th and 18th centuries St. David's was home for whalers, in fact whaling started here before the rest of the New World.

IN THE HARBOR OF ST. GEORGE'S

The harbour of the oldest English settlement still existing in the western hemisphere is small and colorful. The picture shows Ordnance Island with a colorful ship in the foreground.

Page 75

ST. PETER'S CHURCH, ST. GEORGE'S

St. Peter's is the oldest Anglican church in continuous use in the New World. The first wooden church was built by the first governor, Richard Moore, in 1612, but a more substantial building was erected here in 1619. The church was rebuilt again in its present form in 1713 and enlarged in 1814. The cedar altar has been in use since 1624. The lower picture shows some of the old graves at the church.

Page 76

17TH CENTURY SHIP *DELIVERANCE*

The Deliverance *and her consort, the* Patience, *were built by survivors of the* Sea Venture *and carried them safely to Jamestown ten months after the shipwreck. On the St. George's waterfront at Ordnance Island is a superb replica of the* Deliverance.

FORT ST. CATHERINE AND BEACH

This view shows to the right the beautiful St. Catherine's Beach. To the left is Fort St. Catherine, reaching out into the Atlantic. Construction began on Fort St. Catherine in 1613 and continued in the eighteenth and nineteenth centuries until 1880, when Bermuda had become the «Gibraltar of the West». Never was a shot fired in anger from this massive fortification, which is open to the public.

ON SHELLY BAY, HAMILTON PARISH

Shelly Bay is one of the lively points on the North Shore of Bermuda. In the foreground is one of Bermuda's popular moongates.

IN THE BERMUDA AQUARIUM (Flatts Inlet)

Founded in 1926 by L.L. Mowbray, the Aquarium is on the edge of a tideway, boiling alternately in and out of Harrington Sound. Surface water is pumped from this tideway into the Aquarium and in its twenty-seven tanks. About seventy species of Bermuda reef fish are on display. Active pelagic fishes like barracuda, jacks and sharks can be seen in the large 40,000-gallon reef tank.

THE PEPPERCORN CEREMONY, ST. GEORGE'S

When the government moved from St. George's to Hamilton in 1816, the State House was rented to Bermuda's oldest Masonic Lodge, St. George, under the Scottish constitution charter dated August 7, 1797. The annual rental is one peppercorn. The payment of this rent has become the occasion for a most colorful ceremony. The date was formerly December 27, the Feast of St. John the Evangelist. Later it was changed to fall on the most convenient date nearest April 23, St. George's Day.

BERMUDA PAGEANTRY

There are many functions and ceremonies in Bermuda in keeping with old traditions. The Speaker of the House of Assembly appears in white wig and old costume.

There are colorful ceremonies in winter especially. A highlight in Hamilton is the "Skirling Ceremony", held in Fort Hamilton. At noon, kilted pipers and drummers perform on the ramparts of the fort, which commands a breathtaking view of the city, the harbor, and the island.

Every Wednesday from November to March, the mayor of St. George's personally greets visitors to the old town, and there is a walking tour of the historic area, which is repeated on Saturdays. And, every Wednesday throughout the year, the Town Crier leads a Ducking Stool punishment, with a volunteer visitor in 17th-century garb being lowered squealing into the harbor.

The opening of the Parliament also means a big parade, with His Excellency the Governor and Commander-in-Chief inspecting the formations.

THE OLD RECTORY, ST. GEORGE'S

This romantic National Trust cottage is a gem of early Bermuda architecture. It was the home of George Dew, a pardoned pirate of the early eighteenth century, who became a respected citizen of St. George's.

Midcentury it became the rectory, when the Reverend Alexander Richardson married the widowed lady whose home it was.

Page 81

TYPICAL BERMUDA ROOF, ST. GEORGE'S

The roofs of most of the Bermuda houses are made of native limestone. They are constructed of inch-thick slates laid over a stone gutter at the angle appropriate for the purpose of leading every drop of rainwater into a water tank beneath the house. Each household is responsible for its own water supply. The picture shows the roof of an old Bermuda house, built in 1725, now the Historical Society Museum.

Page 82

HISTORICAL HOUSES IN ST. GEORGE'S

Upper left: Tucker House
Left: Confederate Museum
Upper right: Joseph Stockade
   House
Historical Society Museum

The Tucker House on Water Street,
built in the eighteenth century, was the home of Henry Tucker, colonial secretary of Bermuda during the American Revolution. It is open to the public and has a fine collection of antique furnishings.

The Confederate Museum
on Duke of York Street was built by Governor Samuel Day in 1699 in

the garden of the old Government House as his private residence. It was later converted into a hotel and was used during the American Civil War as the headquarters of the Confederate agents. It was the hub of high adventure in the days of blockade-running out of Bermuda.

msp 6

Situated on Printers Alley, this was the house of Joseph Stockdale, who in 1783 brought the first printing press to Bermuda. He was the founder of the Bermuda Gazette, *Bermuda's first newspaper.*

Historical Society Museum

Housed in a picturesque old house built in 1725 on Featherbed Alley, the museum shows how Bermudians lived in the early days. The hand-carved Bermuda cedar table in the living room was used 350 years ago in the old State House. There is a letter from General George Washington, dated in 1775, asking for gunpowder from Bermuda, and copies of the Royal Gazette *from 1784. (See also picture on page 81.)*

Page 83

ST. GEORGE'S TOWN HALL

Dominating King's Square, the Town Hall, meeting place of the Town Corporation, was built in 1808 beside a building erected in 1782. It has recently been restored, with Bermuda cedar used extensively for the woodwork.

THE OLD BRIDGE HOUSE

Just behind the Town Hall is the old Bridge House, so called because there was once a bridge here over a lagoon that divided the town. The lagoon was filled in to become Somers Garden. Bridge House was once a governor's residence. Edward Goodrich bought it in 1787 from his brother, Bridger. Both brothers owned several privateers during the French wars.

Page 84

CHURCH RUINS, ST. GEORGE'S

This church on Duke of Kent Street was to have replaced St. Peter's, the historical Anglican parish church, which was badly in need of repair. The foundations of the new church, planned as a magnificent example of Victorian Gothic, were laid in 1874, but it was never finished. Money ran low, and interest in restoring St. Peter's revived. And so today flowers and bushes are the church's only congregation, and birds its choir.

Page 85

TUCKER'S TOWN BAY

Tucker's Town on the southeastern coast of Bermuda was founded in the hope that it would become the capital of Bermuda. With Castle Harbour as a perfect approach from the ocean, it would have been a fine location. But the capital was moved from St. George's to Hamilton. Today Tucker's Town is one of the most exclusive and elegant

residential sections of Bermuda, with a fine white-sand beach on the South Shore, a safe harbour, and two of the best golf courses, Castle Harbour and Mid Ocean.

FISHING IS GOOD IN BERMUDA

Shore, reef, and deep-sea fishing are all great around Bermuda. There are plenty of bonefish, pompano, and gray snapper along the shore. Amberjack, yellowtail, chub, and rockfish live among the coral reefs. Blue and white marlin, blackfin tuna, Allison tuna, dolphin, wahoo, and bonito are caught in the deep waters surrounding the islands.

Page 86

NATURAL ARCHES, TUCKER'S TOWN

The coast of Bermuda has many dramatic and unusual rock formations. The Natural Arches on the beach at Tucker's Town are a spectacular feature developed from caves on the edge of the ocean and opened up by waves.

MARRIOTT'S CASTLE HARBOUR RESORT

The centers of social activity around Tucker's Town are the Mid Ocean Club and Marriott's Castle Harbour Resort, one of the most elegant hotels of the islands, with two swimming pools, an eighteen-hole championship golf course, beautiful gardens, private beach, and tennis courts.

Page 87

CASTLE HARBOUR GOLF CLUB (First Hole)

The first hole at Castle Harbour is the most scenic opener of any on Bermuda's seven links. Looking down from the attractive new club house, the picture shows the beautiful view of the golf course with the brilliant blue-green waters of Castle Harbour to the left. In the background, deep blue, is the Atlantic Ocean. The eighteen-hole course has a total yardage of 6,142.

CASTLE ISLAND BEACH

Far east on the Castle Roads connecting the ocean with Castle Harbour is Castle Island, known for its strong fortifications, the King's Castle, and the notorious Black Hole. Here also is a romantic beach, shown in the picture.

Page 88

CRYSTAL CAVES

Bermuda's most beautiful caves are in the narrow strip of land between Harrington Sound and Castle Harbour. Leamington and Crystal Caves are outstanding, real underground wonderlands with stalagmites and stalactites, enhanced by crystal-clear pools of the subterranean fairyland.

Page 89

NIGHT LIFE IN BERMUDA

Native singers and musicians are a feature of night life in Bermuda, where the balmy evenings allow outside entertainment all year round.

THE ROYAL NAVAL DOCKYARD ON IRELAND ISLAND

Once a key British naval base, today this houses Bermuda's Maritime Museum, as well as a marina, restaurants, a shopping center, an art gallery and several businesses. The museum houses exhibitions which chronicle Bermuda's association with the Royal Navy and its long maritime history.

Pages 90-91

MID OCEAN GOLD CLUB

Mid Ocean Club, which winds around Tucker's Town, is ranked among the top ten golf courses in the world by experts. Designed in 1924 by Charles Blair MacDonald and revised in 1953 by Robert Trent Jones, Mid Ocean's eighteen holes measure 6,519 yards and offer beautiful views over the ocean and romantic Tucker's Town.

EASTER LILIES AT THE BERMUDA PERFUMERY

Fields of blooming Easter lilies cover Bermuda in April and May. Brought from China in the nineteenth century to Bermuda, they grew so well that they were soon being grown all over the islands.

Page 92

PALM GROVE GARDEN (Devonshire)

The flower gardens of Bermuda are unique. The picture shows part of a private garden on South Road in

Devonshire that is open to the public and is noted for the variety of its arrangement.

Page 93
NORTH COAST AT THE CRAWL
The North Coast of Bermuda is wildly romantic, a rocky coast with small beaches protected in bays and inlets. This is a view to the north along the rough ocean coast of Hamilton Parish, with homes and a school perched on Crawl Hill.

Page 94
HISTORIC FLATTS INLET
This is one of the loveliest and most peaceful points of Bermuda. Here the waters of the Atlantic ebb and flow through Flatts Inlet to feed Harrington Sound, an almost completely land-locked body of water where water sports abound. Flatts was one of Bermuda's leading ports in the early eighteenth century, and was an important center for the colony.

RENTAL TRANSPORTATION
Out of a desire to avoid too much traffic in the delightful narrow streets and roads of the islands, there are no rental cars in Bermuda. There is a good bus system and taxis, bicycles, mopeds and scooters (see picture) can be rented by visitors. The photograph shows a typical street scene, with the policeman directing traffic wearing Bermuda shorts, just as the tourists do.

Page 95
SOUTH SHORE AT TUCKER'S TOWN
The air view shows the wide sandy beaches at the east end of the South Shore with the beach of Castle Harbour Hotel. Visible above the beaches are the two golf courses Mid Ocean and Castle Harbour.

TOM MOORE'S TAVERN
One of the oldest homes in Bermuda is charming «Walsingham», built by Samuel Trott, kinsman of the Earl of Warwick, and located between Leamington and Crystal Caves. Tom Moore, the poet, visited here in 1804, and described the garden in one of his poems. «Walsingham» is now a gourmet restaurant called «Tom Moore's» after the poet.

Page 96
A BERMUDA SUNSET
The sunsets are unforgettable, with the reflection of brilliant colors in the water. Bermuda's way of life is such that nearly every house has a verandah, terrace, or patio where one can entertain friends, have meals, or simply relax and watch the sea, the fleecy clouds, and the sunset.

Continued from Page 72

a specialist to determine that much of this sand is shelly in origin. Sift it through your fingers on the beach and you will see the shell particles. Because of the prevailing winds and waves, the South Shore is the sandiest. Coral reefs contribute their share of sand to the land also, and much of the beauty to the waters around Bermuda. Coral grows in the shallow waters off land masses in the tropical and subtropical world, and nowhere farther north than Florida around the continental United States today. But living coral grows around Bermuda. The reefs protect the land, shelter the fish, and delight undersea explorers.

The warm Gulf Stream that crosses the Atlantic nearby is responsible for this blessing. Along the South Shore of Bermuda are coral atolls known as "pot boilers." The living coral rises around the rim of the atoll in a circle, and the sunken hollow in the center has been worn by circulating water into the underlying limestone.

In terms of geological eras, the North Shore of Bermuda is youthful, the South Shore mature. The youthful coast is steep, rocky, not worn away by sea and wind. The mature coast has been planed smooth by time and tide and has sandy shores deposited by the ocean in past millennia.

CAVES, COVES, AND COAST

Bermuda's limestone is honeycombed with caves, underground amphitheaters with floors almost one hundred feet beneath the surface of the land. In the shapes sculptured by nature and in the coloring of the formations and deposits within the caves, they are a delight to the eye and the imagination. Transparently clear salt water pools have been formed in the caves by seepage and underground passages to the sea. Some are open to the public and have electric lights showing the way into the caverns. Many more are on land not open to the public and are hidden by vegetation.

The geological account of the formation of these caves is more fascinating than any myth, for measurements indicate that some have been far more than half a million years in the making; the sea has risen and fallen several times during their creation. They have been carved from the rock by that percolating, slightly acid water that dissolves the limestone, as most caves have been created in other regions of the world. The water has eaten away one part of the stone and not another, because some of the stone is harder, denser, and more tightly cemented than are other adjacent strata of rock.

It is also evident in some parts of the island that hollow sand pockets exist under the cap of limestone. The softer rock and the sand have been washed out, in a process that went on more rapidly during the Ice Ages than it does now. During those times much more of the ocean's waters were locked in the ice caps that spread out from both poles. The seas of the world fell far below the level at which they now stand, not once but several times. More rain fell in that cold time. Bermuda was more elevated above the sea, so the washing out of soft stone and sandy pockets under the stone cap went on more rapidly then than it does now.

After the caves were formed, they were adorned with stalactites and stalagmites. The water would drip down into a cavern ever so slowly; as a drop fell from the roof, it left behind a little of the lime dissolved in it. When it landed on the floor of the cave, it deposited a little lime before evaporating or flowing away to the sea. In that way stalactites and stalagmites were formed, as ages wheeled past. A stalactite hangs down from the ceiling of the caves, like a flow of water suddenly turned to stone in mid-air. A stalagmite grows up from the floor of the caves as the lime crystallizes out of the fallen water.

Not only are the shapes of the dripping stone exotic, the coloring is also most beautiful and the surfaces often sensuously smooth to the touch. Some stones are pale white, others are red or tinged with green from iron or copper dissolved in the waters that formed them.

Some of the caves have been rich in finds of fossil birds. A study of the fossil bones shows that the birds had been unable to fly when they were alive.

Among the dramatic big caves that are open to the public are the Crystal Caves in Hamilton Parish, near the Causeway. The underground scenery is well lighted with electric lights, and steps have been cut in the rocks. The stalactites drip from the roof into Crystal Lake, a clear pool of salt water that rises and falls with the tide and is about thirty feet deep at the height of the incoming sea. A pontoon bridge allows the explorer to enjoy the whole stone forest of stalactites and stalagmites.

Nearby are a number of other caverns —Leamington Cave, Cahow Cave, Castle Grotto, Blue Hole, and Fern Cave. Another is Cathedral Cave, with a mighty stalagmite that looks like an organ pipe. Leamington Cave is near Harrington Sound and just off Sound Road. With its arched dome more than sixty feet underground, it is truly out of this world. This double-chambered cave is also well lighted. In Castle Grotto Cave the visitor can enjoy the glittering roof above the fish-filled waters of its pool, Blue Hole.

Fascinating evidence of the ages that it took to create the great caves is found in the record of a stalagmite from Walsingham Cave. This huge stone column, eleven feet high, was cut in 1819 and sent to a museum in Edinburgh, Scotland. A measurement made years later of the tiny new stalagmites forming on the stump of the big one indicated that, at the rate they were growing, it took 600,000 years of dripping to create the stalagmite taken from Bermuda to Scotland.

When a cave becomes geologically old, it may collapse, and what is left has its own special fascination. The roof falls in, leaving arches of rock, strange columns, and limpid pools of great beauty, known prosaically as sinks. The death of a cave formed the dramatic natural arch of rock near the Mid-Ocean Club at Tucker's Town beside the beach. The islands are graced with all sorts of fantastic natural rock sculpture that originated in the collapse of caves, and the land near the shores is dotted with clear sinks filled with salt water that enters through underground passages or through seepage. Cathedral Rocks is a noble ruin of a natural temple formed during the process of cave-making and cave-dying, with the added help of wave erosion.

One of them, Devil's Hole, has been one of Bermuda's most distinctive attractions for more than a century. It is a land-locked, crystal-clear, salt-water pool filled with fish —a natural aquarium. There is apparently no connection between the waters of Devil's Hole, which are about thirty feet deep, and nearby Harrington Sound, and presumably the sea fills this marine pool through an undersea channel from the South Shore of the island.

Here, more than a thousand strange and beautiful fish serenely glide through the clear waters, thronging to the surface when they are fed. Angel Fish, grouper, rockfish, and many other colorful reef fish make their home here. Visitors are allowed to fish for them—with a baited line but without a hook. Devil's Hole earned its name because of the strange growling noise that the water makes at very low tide when, probably, it passes underground between the sink and the sea. The word has, quite naturally, become "Go to Devil's Hole and see the Angel Fish." Like other sinks, it was once a large cave, as stalactites and stalagmites attest, and in its present form was created when the roof caved in.

The reefs and patches of coral near the coasts are another source of great pleasure, especially in these days of SCUBA diving and undersea tourism. The coral canyons are home to a multitude of fish and other sea creatures, and purple sea fans wave. To float above the canyons on the surface of the water and watch this world through a face mask is to be relaxed. To dive is to explore a beauty the land cannot offer. For those who don't want to get wet, there are glass-bottomed boats to take them to the sea gardens near the coast.

THE CLIMATE

The climate is the chief asset of Bermuda, making it a haven for refugees from winter. It is so breeze-washed that sun-lovers enjoy it in the summer, too. Warmed by the nearby Gulf Stream, the islands have not had a frost since official weather records have been kept. Sunstroke is also unknown here.

The surrounding ocean warms the specks of land in the winter and cools them in the summer. The climate is subtropical, though Bermuda is opposite Cape Hatteras in North Carolina. South Florida can get colder than Bermuda has ever been. There is not a great range of temperature throughout the year. The lowest temperature ever officially recorded in Bermuda was 41 degrees. The average temperature in August, the hottest month, is 80 degrees, and in February, the coolest, 62 degrees. The bitter winter cold fronts that move from Canada and New England over the ocean toward Bermuda are warmed by the Gulf Stream before they reach the islands, where they bring rain but never snow.

The weather of Bermuda does change, and in a delightful fashion. After several clear blue days, cumulus clouds tower high, sweep across the land, and shed showers, and then the sun comes out again and a fresh, air-conditioning breeze springs up. There is nothing dull or listless about the weather. Connoisseurs of skyscapes are among Bermuda's most devoted lovers. The frequent changes in winds and the brief, heavy rain showers are brought about by the great pattern of winds that prevails in the Atlantic.

A dominant weather feature of the Atlantic is the "Azores-Bermuda high." This "high" is an air mass composed of winds circulating clockwise around a high-pressure center. The high-pressure system normally lies over the ocean between Bermuda and the Azores, and its movement gives Bermuda its refreshing changes in weather. Movement of the high-pressure system north and south determines Bermuda's winds and showers, and the high is so situated that Bermuda frequently lies in what is called a zone of convergence. In this zone the trade winds blowing from the east that dominate the ocean south of Bermuda meet the winds coming from the west that have crossed the continent of North America.

The pattern of weather in the summer depends on the movement of the high-pressure system lying over the ocean to the east. When the high moves toward the Azores, the easterly trade winds curve round it and bring to Bermuda clear and sunny days and bright blue skies. Then, usually, the high migrates again, and the winds shift toward the south, bringing high clouds and rain showers. It is the convergence of winds from the high-pressure system with those of a low-pressure system moving toward Bermuda from the west that produces the frequent showers. The prevailing winds of the islands are from the south, southwest, and west. The occasional storms with high winds that pass over Bermuda come in the fall. Bermuda has a yearly average of 7.1 hours of sunshine a day. Though the air is moist, the average humidity is less than that of Britain. There is no dry season in the islands, and the brief, heavy rains refresh the land throughout the year. There is no rainy season, either, no periods when one is shut in all day. The welcome rain keeps the islands emerald green, and Bermudians catch some of it to store in stone reservoirs or tanks for their water supply. The entire absence of fog over the islands is one of the most welcome aspects of the climate. There are no heat waves. The sea temperature is warmer than the land in the winter, cooler in the summer. The outdoor life is pleasant all the year round.

Because of the benign weather, visitors have been going to Bermuda to recuperate from illnesses, including nervous prostration, since before the time there was a United States. The cold of the northeastern United States and Canada, which brought on pneumonia, could be avoided here, and English colonists in North America quickly learned this. It did not take the English long, either, to realize that the climate of Bermuda is kinder than that of the Riviera and other Mediterranean lands. The islands are also a refuge for those suffering from hay fever.

Relaxing is the word for a land where warm rains nurture roses and violets in midwinter.

VEGETATION OF BERMUDA

The first settlers of Bermuda found a dense covering of vegetation, with the famous cedar trees dominating the landscape. The subtropical forests and swamps were lush. Wind, water, and birds carried the seeds of the first plants to the specks of land soon after they rose above the sea.

The fragrant Bermuda cedar, a species of juniper, is an evergreen tree. It grows both on rock and on fertile soils. Because the wood is superior for boatbuilding and for furniture-making, it was highly valued and heavily timbered. However, since 1945 most of the Bermuda cedars have been killed by a scale pest, in spite of strenuous attempts to eradicate the disease. New cedars are growing, and there is hope for a revival.

Seeds of the palmetto tree were also brought in by natural agencies in the distant past, and the first colonists found these tall and striking emigrants from the southern part of the United States raising their distinctive crowns on the islands. The colonists not only ate the delectable heart of the palmetto and used its leaves to thatch their shelters, they also used the palmetto sap to make a potent fermented alcoholic drink called "bibby." Not nearly so many palmettos are found on Bermuda today as once flourished there, but they can be seen on the North Shore in Palmetto Park, around Paget Marsh, and in Devonshire on the South Shore.

The bay grape, also called the sea grape, is one of the most handsome of Bermuda's native trees. Its seeds are viable in salt water, and they grow on the dunes of many tropical and subtropical lands. It has large, shiny, almost round leaves and a handsome, many-branching trunk with a thin bark that varies from red to brown. The "grapes" that hang from these trees in the fall are not particularly tasty, but a good jelly can be made from them.

Another native tree, the mangrove, is strange to northerners but familiar to anyone who has lived in tropical or subtropical climes around the world. The mangrove seed floats in on the tide, drops its heavier end down, and roots on tidal flats. It requires some salt in the water in which it grows. The glossy-leafed trees put out many, many roots into the air and then down into the water and the soil. These roots catch sand and silt and bind them down, so the trees have a great reputation as land builders in warm climates. The waters that flow about their roots are nurseries for all sorts of infant sea creatures. Mangrove blooms make an excellent honey.

The purple morning-glory vines grow luxuriantly over the wastelands of the islands and can strangle trees. One of the most attractive of the native Bermuda plants is the Bermudiana, a small thing with lovely blue flowers bearing a yellow eye. It resembles the iris and blooms profusely on rocky hillsides and near sandy shores in early summer. There is also a maidenhair fern that has become abundant on walls and cliffs. Magnificent giant ferns with stalks five feet long are found in some marshes. The Spanish bayonet is another native plant, easy to identify. It has many

long, stiff, heavy leaves, bearing sharp points, and most dramatic and delicate white blooms that contrast sharply with the stiff plant.

Over the centuries since men first settled on the islands, the vegetation of Bermuda has, of course, changed. The heavy mantle of cedar has gone, but much that is beautiful has been added. This is because the climate has been hospitable to both temperate and tropical plants. Oleanders, originally from the Mediterranean but introduced from South Carolina, casuarina trees from Australia, roses from China—all are at home there now. Bananas, coconut palms, royal poincianas, royal palms, passion flowers, Easter lilies, orange trees, peach trees all thrive. Bamboo graces the landscape frequently. Pungent lantana grows wild. Some cactus is native to the island, other decorative varieties have been introduced and grow well. One of the most beautiful members of the cactus family is the night-blooming cereus, which bears a magnificent and fragrant flower that never lasts beyond the dawn. Mimosas and acacias have made themselves at home, growing well even when neglected. Poinsettias bloom outdoors at Christmas time (if the plants have been pruned at the proper time). Hibiscus shrubs add the bright notes of their red, pink, and yellow flowers to the landscape and are prized as hedges. Many species of ficus trees thrive, and the rubber tree is one of them.

The most distinctive thing about the vegetation of Bermuda, to visitors from colder climates, is that there is no fall, no winter, no time of bare, gray branches. The leaves of the trees and shrubs and vines

Cedar Avenue, Hamilton, 1885

are pushed off after new leaves have grown. It is an evergreen world. Both to the botanist interested in introducing plants from other parts of the world and to the gardener with a green thumb, Bermuda is a delectable part of the world, for a great variety of vegetation will do well there, given the proper care.

The Famous Bermuda Flower Gardens

Because Bermuda has proved to be as hospitable to trees and flowers of the world as it is to people, the gardens are a joy.

Here the beloved blooms of England, the roses and delphiniums, thrive alongside orchids and begonias. Because Bermudians and their visitors live outdoors the year round, gardens are greatly cherished as outdoor living rooms.

For decades one of the most beautiful sights on the islands has been the vast expanse of Easter lilies that are grown for export. First it was the bulbs that were raised for the market, back in the nineteenth century, Later, but before the days of air freight, blooms were shipped. Today, in the jet age, not only lilies but many other flowers are flown to market in the northeastern United States. The open fields of flowers that bloom when frost still threatens on the North American continent are breathtaking.

The great variety of native and imported decorative trees and plants can be seen in the Public Garden at St. George's and at the Agricultural Station at Paget. The traditional English love for gardening has also resulted in enriching the landscape. Sea captains brought back roses from the Orient, begonias from Mexico, orchids from Central America, Mexico, the West Indies, and Asia. If the right species of orchid is selected for a Bermuda garden, it demands less attention than many other plants. Calendula thrive here. Date palms grow well. Honeysuckle perfumes the air. Nasturtiums and passion flowers are among the favorites.

All gardeners, it has been said, plant the gardens of their memories. That is why so many of the blooming borders and beds that grace Bermuda gardens evoke England and New England. But there is a hunger, too, among those who love a world in bloom, to experiment with new and exotic color and fragrance. One of the favorite imported trees that have become domesticated on the islands is the royal poinciana, also known as flamboyante. It is a handsome shade tree in summer, with its high umbrella-shaped crown and lacy little green leaves. In May it bursts into bloom and is like a fountain of flame.

Backyard fruit gardens are also found throughout the islands. Bananas, grapefruit, oranges, avocadoes, peaches, and loquats are grown for home consumption.

ROSES IN BERMUDA

The early settlers brought roses to Bermuda, and the clipper ships of the nineteenth century brought back magnificent roses from China, along with tea and spices. There has been much traffic in roses and in their commercial propagation in Bermuda. New varieties introduced into Britain and America soon found their way to Bermuda. A number of roses have become horticultural escapes. Multiflora roses climb over old walls. Some of the old, old roses of England are still grown, alongside species from China and newer hybrids, and the Cherokee rose is naturalized in Bermuda.

THE POPULATION

Though Bermuda has a comparatively dense population per acre, the homes of the islands have spread out rather than going up in high-rise construction. There are still many hilly areas that are free of habitations. No aborigines were living here when the English colonists arrived, and the people are largely of English, Portuguese, and African descent. Negroes are in the majority, forming about three-fifths of the population. The relations between the blacks and the whites have been so pleasant that many West Indian Negroes have chosen to move to Bermuda in this century. More and more, people from Canada and North America who come to Bermuda to visit are buying or building retirement homes.

Hamilton, the capital, is Bermuda's largest city. The site in the center of the islands was chosen for its ease of access, and the city rises delightfully on the hill above sheltered Hamilton Harbour. The city continues to grow in a well-planned fashion and preserves its eighteenth-century charm. It is a busy town, as the center of government, the principal market place, and the location of most of the businesses of Bermuda. St. George, on the eastern end, is the second largest and historically the most interesting of Bermuda's towns. Its small winding streets make for delightful strolls.

Homes in Bermuda tend to be strung along the main roads that link the islands, or clustered in small villages on the shore, like Flatts Village. Though there is still considerable farming, there are few isolated farmhouses. Farmers go out from neighborly settlements to work their tracts of land.

Bermudians have a strong affection for English tradition and the symbolism and pomp of other days. They celebrate Empire Day, Guy Fawkes Day and the Queen's Birthday. They have lived for so long at a major marine crossroads of the world, and so many have ranged the world that they are by no means insular in spirit. They are descended from a breed that has mastered seafaring, farming and trading. They can best be described as gracious and hospitable conservatives who know how to govern themselves competently and enjoy life.

A delightful example of the way that Bermudians preserve colorful traditions is the annual Peppercorn Ceremony, complete with the trooping of the colors by the Bermuda Regiment and gold-braided and top-hatted dignitaries. The occasion is the payment of the year's annual rent of Masonic Lodge St. George Number 266. The ceremony first took place in 1816, when the capital of the Bermuda government was moved to Hamilton from St. George. The

State House at St. George's was then granted in trust to the Masonic Lodge. Each year the mayor of St. George's welcomes the governor of Bermuda to the Peppercorn Ceremony, and the governor then demands and receives the key to the State House. One peppercorn is paid in rent. The ceremony is now held on the most convenient day nearest April 23, St. George's Day.

Other traditions were brought to the islands from Africa, whose folklore is reflected in the dancing of the Gombeys, colorfully dressed groups that parade and drum on Easter Monday and Boxing Day. From the West Indies have come steel drums and calypso.

BERMUDA TODAY

There is no problem in visiting Bermuda today, except most visitors must remember to drive on the lefthand side of the road. Frequent jet flights are scheduled to the islands from England, Canada, and the United States. There are also frequent cruise ships. Official identification (passport or certified birth certificate) of U.S. citizenship is required of U.S. citizens.

The local currency is on a par with the U.S. dollar, which is accepted everywhere. There are excellent overseas phone and cable services between Bermuda and the rest of the world. Transportation by taxi, bicycle, bus, moped, carriage and ferry is easy to obtain.

Complete facilities and equipment for just about every outdoor sport may be found here. They play cricket in Bermuda from May through September, and soccer from October through April. There are over 100 tennis courts, including public courts at the Bermuda Tennis Stadium. Horse-back riding is available.

In the water world, there are cruises to the Sea Gardens in glass-bottom boats. Sightseeing on the water is also done by catamaran and motor-yacht cruises. Sail-boats, ranging from small Sunfish to larger yachts with a licensed skipper, are for hire. To explore the beautiful underwater world of the coral reefs there are snorkel tours, SCUBA diving tours, and helmet diving tours. Water skiing can also be enjoyed.

All sorts of night-time entertainment enliven the evenings, from motion pictures

Hamilton, 1885

to exciting night clubs and lavish floor shows in some of the hotels. Free-port shopping, with luxurious articles from all over the world, makes Hamilton a shopper's paradise.

Some of the most modern and luxurious resort hotels, clubs, and cottage colonies in the world receive visitors to Bermuda. They range from casual, informal, and inexpensive to formal and quite expensive. Many private homes take guests.

Among the best places are these:

Large Resort Hotels: Belmont Hotel and Golf Club, Elbow Beach, Grotto Bay Beach, Harmony Club, Hamilton Princess, Marriott's Castle Harbour Resort, Mermaid Beach, Princess (Hamilton), Sonesta Beach, Southampton Princess, and Stonington Beach.

Small Hotels: Glencoe, Newstead, Palmetto Hotel and Cottages, Pompano Beach Club, The Reefs, Rosedon, Royal Palms Club, Waterloo House and White Sands.

Clubs: Coral Beach and Tennis Club, and Mid-Ocean Club.

Cottage Colonies: Ariel Sands, Cambridge Beaches, Horizons, Lantana, Pink Beach and Willowbank.

Guest Houses, and Large House-keeping Cottages and Apartments: Angels Grotto Apartments, Barnsdale Guest Apartments, Brightside Guest Apartments, Cabana Vacation Apartments, Greenbank Guest House and Cottages, Hillcrest Guest House, Loughlands, Marley Beach, Mermaid West, Munro Beach, Pretty Penny, Rosemont, Royal Palms Club, Salt Kettle House, Sky-Top Cottages, South Capers, Surf Side Beach, White Heron, and Woodbourne/Inverness.

Sightseeing: HAMILTON

Strolling the streets of Hamilton has been a pleasure to visitors since they first began coming to the islands. Overlooking the city is the Sessions House, built in 1817 shortly after Hamilton became the capital. It is rich in history. Here the Bermuda Parliament meets, and public galleries in the meeting chambers allow visitors to observe the sessions. There are older buildings dating back to the eighteenth century still in use, as well as a number of new office buildings—a tribute to the increasing numbers of off-shore company offices established in the island. Many old houses still stand in Hamilton; Par-la-Ville is one. It now shelters the public library and the Bermuda Historical Society Museum. In the lovely Par-la-Ville garden grows a hundred-year-old rubber tree.

The city is dominated by the Bermuda Cathedral (Anglican), which is set on a ridge together with the handsome City Hall. The City Hall is a civic center for the island, containing the National Gallery, the Bermuda Society of Arts Gallery and Bermuda's best theater. The Public Building, set in a park between Reid and Front Streets, houses the Cabinet Office and the Senate Chamber as well as many historical items. Fort Hamilton, with its moat full of native trees and shrubs, is well worth visiting.

Bermuda Cathedral, Hamilton

... TO THE WEST

A ferry trip to Somerset and Ireland Island is a pleasant way to visit the western part of Bermuda. Ireland Island once held a mighty British Dockyard, and today the Royal Navy still retains a small base, but most of the splendid buildings are used for small shops, light factories and boatworks, and the Bermuda Maritime Museum. The Museum contains treasures found on Bermuda's reefs and has displays about the island's long maritime history and connection with the Royal Navy.

If you are renting a moped or scooter take it with you on the ferry and get off at one of the Somerset Island stops. There are many charming by-ways and a beautiful shore-line, and some fine examples of old Bermudian architecture. The drive back from there leads first to the southwest and around the western end of the chain of islands, and then curves eastward along the South Shore, past Gibb's Hill Lighthouse, which is open to visitors. Along the South Shore Road are views of the finest beaches in Bermuda, and some of the best hotels, club and cottage colonies.

...TO THE EAST

To the east of Hamilton on the South Shore Road lie diverse attractions. The botanical gardens in Paget Parish are excellent. Verdmont, in Smith's Parish, is an elegant eighteenth-century house that was completely restored by the Bermuda National Trust. Also see Spanish Rock, Spittal Pond, and the Devil's Hole, all beautiful scenic places along the South Shore Road. Tucker's Town is the luxurious residential section through which the golf course of the Mid Ocean Club winds. Nearby on the beach are weird natural rock arches.

North of Tucker's Town, as the road swings round Harrington Sound, are Crystal Caves and Leamington Caves, open to the public. The road continues around the sound and follows the North Shore, reaching Flatts Village by way of a small bridge across the inlet from the sea to Harrington Sound. In this part of the island is the Bermuda Aquarium, Museum and Zoo. The Aquarium contains many fascinating species and the Museum tells much about Bermuda's natural history. The Zoo has a number of tropical birds and several giant tortoises brought from the Galapagos Islands.

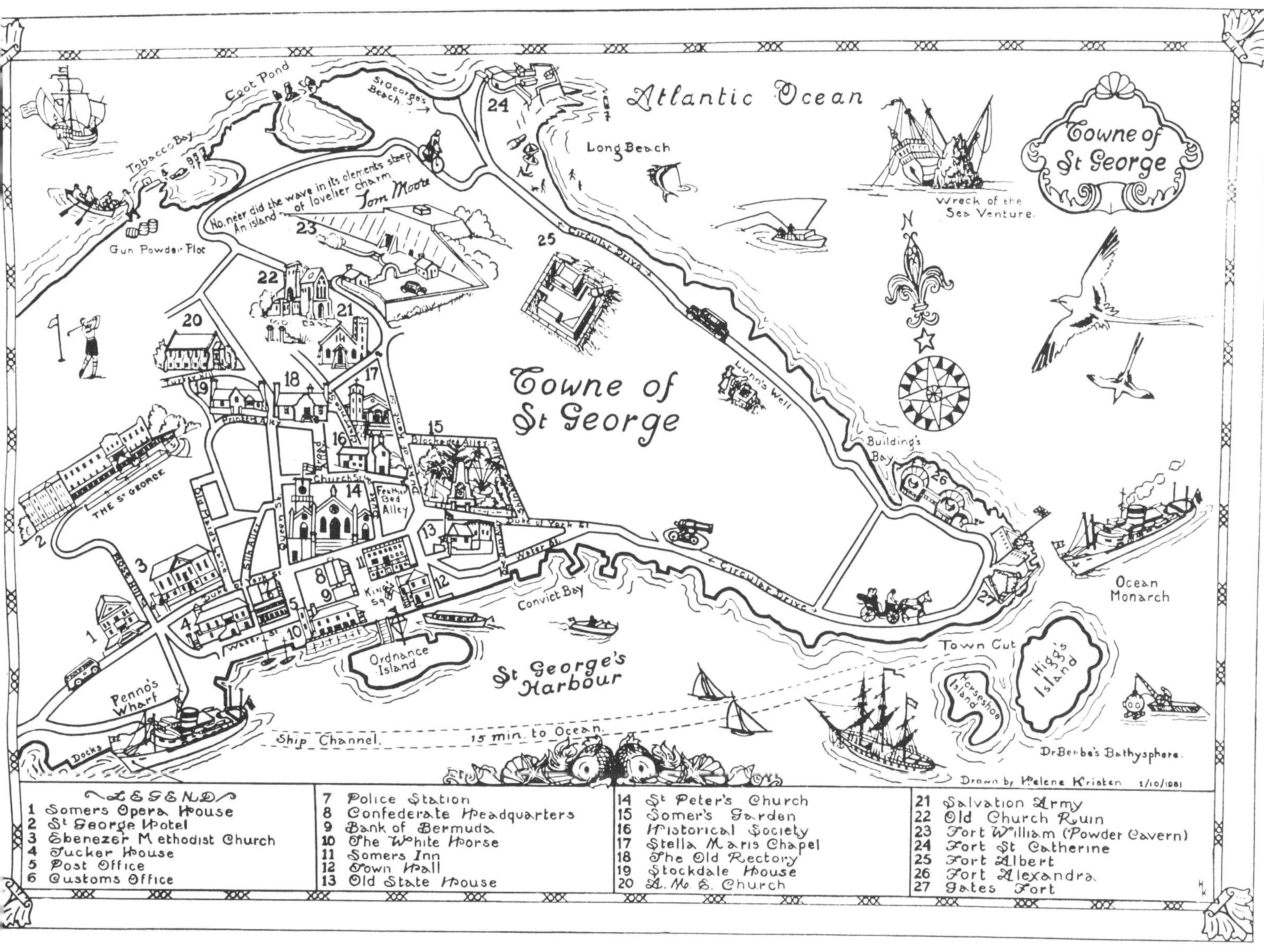

Map of St. George's drawn by Helene Kristen, 1951

ST. GEORGE'S

A visit to St. George's is a step far back in time. Founded in 1612, the first capital slept for more than a century after the government was moved to Hamilton. Here is the State House, the oldest stone building on Bermuda, now rented to the Freemasons for an annual rent of one peppercorn. Exploring the winding, narrow lanes by foot is the way to see St. George's. St. Peter's Church on York Street, the oldest Anglican church in the western world, was built in 1713 on the site of the first wooden church, which had been built in 1612. The Old Rectory, was once the home of a reformed pirate. Old Maid's Lane is where Tom Moore lived and flirted with his neighbor's wife. In Somers Garden on Duke of York Street, the heart of Sir George Somers, founder of Bermuda, is buried. A number of beautifully restored old houses are open to the public.

Near St. George's are Bermuda's oldest forts—Gates' Fort, built in 1612, and Fort St. Catherine, dating from 1613. On the southern side of St. George's Harbour is U.S. Naval Air Station, with Bermuda's Civil Air Terminal at its western end. On the extreme eastern tip of the land is St. David's Island, whose population is said to be descended from Negro, Indian, and Irish ancestors. There is a grand view from St. David's Lighthouse on St. David's Head, the finish line for the Newport to Bermuda Ocean Yacht Race.

FISHING

Bermuda is a favorite base for sports fishermen, for it offers great angling along the shore, above the coral reefs, and in the deep, blue waters around the islands. A fleet of fine charter boats is based here, at Somerset, Southampton, Pembroke, Paget, Smith's Parish, and St. George's. They are well equipped, with outriggers, fighting chairs, and experienced crews. The fishing season now runs all year, and during that time some of the best light-tackle fishing anywhere in the world can be found in the surrounding waters.

The Annual Bermuda Game Fishing Tournament starts on January 1 and ends on December 31. The tournament is run under the rules of the Bermuda Game Fishing Association. No entry fee and no fishing licenses are required. There are seven categories of tackle, ranging from 2-pound test to 30-pound test. Bermuda also gives a Certificate of Release for game fish that are let go. The contest is limited to fish taken by amateur fishermen with rod and reel. All fish must be officially entered, and the captain of any charter boat can explain how this is done.

In the deep waters offshore the fisherman who is looking for a fight with the larger game fish can be pretty sure to find one. The real heavyweight here is the Allison tuna, also known as the yellowfin tuna. Tunas are taken offshore either by trolling or by chumming, and nothing in the sea can stage such a battle on light tackle.

Wahoo, the speed demons that are among the top ten game fish of the world, run in mid-May. Some are boated throughout the summer. Then, in September and October, the major run is on, and it is hard not to catch a wahoo at that time. They are hooked near St. George's off the eastern end of the islands, and on Challenger Bank and Argus Bank.

Quite a few record-breaking blackfin tuna, which are great fighters, have been caught off Bermuda. In the water over the banks, world-record amberjack have also been caught. Horse-eye bonito and oceanic bonito put up a good fight. Dolphin (the fish, not the smiling mammal) make an especially thrilling catch because they are so beautiful. "Parting day dies like the dolphin" is an accurate description, for they turn sunset colors before expiring. False albacore is another lively catch found in the deeper waters.

Around the twenty square miles of land in Bermuda lie two hundred square miles of coral reef. The reefs are home to a wide variety of fish. Some put up a great fight, some make great eating. They are a perennial source of pleasure to the light-tackle fishermen in outboard-powered small boats.

Some of the deep-water fish also cruise about the reefs, such as false albacore, amberjack, and horse-eye bonito. Yellowtails and gray snappers are found in abundance. Down on the bottom, living in caves, are groupers, which make a splendid chowder.

Along the shore in shallow water swims one of the world's greatest small-game fish, the bonefish. Fishing for bonefish along the beaches in clear, hip-deep water is the favorite sport of many experienced fishermen. All the beauty of that world is suddenly enlivened by a strike by one of the finest fighters of them all. A number of world-record bonefish have been taken around Bermuda. Another great fish that is often caught from the beach by surf fishermen is the pompano, which frequents the waters along the South Shore. Pompano are not only a gourmet's delight, they put up a brisk fight on light tackle. The gray or mangrove snapper is found lurking along the shore and among the roots of the mangrove trees. The angler who catches one of these fish can consider himself really expert, for they are most wily and suspicious.

GOLFING IN BERMUDA

With due apologies to Scotland, many widely-traveled golfers feel that Bermuda is the most perfect place to pursue their sport. Here the fairways are forever green, and the only complaint about them is that the view along the courses can be distracting. There are eight golf courses on the islands. Only two are private clubs which require an introduction by a member or by a hotel.

The Port Royal Golf Course, which is Bermuda's largest course, is by the sea in Southampton. It is one of two government-owned courses, the other being the Ocean View Golf Course overlooking the North Shore in Devonshire. Port Royal, laid out by golf architect Robert Trent Jones, rivals the Mid Ocean Golf Course, considered by experts to be one of the top ten in the world. The Mid Ocean was designed in 1924 by Charles Blair MacDonald, and revised by Robert Trent Jones in 1953. It winds beside the Atlantic for 6,547 yards compared with Port Royal's 6,565 yards.

The first course on Bermuda was that of Riddell's Bay Golf and Country Club, designed in 1922 by Devereux Emmett. It is so near the ocean that youngsters make money by diving for golf balls. Belmont Golf Club is the second oldest on the islands. The fairways of the eighteen holes beside the Great Sound are fringed with oleanders and casuarinas.

The third largest course on Bermuda is that of the Castle Harbour Golf Club. Its eighteen holes, amidst spectacular scenery, were designed on rolling hills by Charles Banks and redesigned by Robert Trent Jones. The Princess Golf and Beach Club has an eighteen-hole executive course on high ground that is well watered and in perfect shape throughout the year. It was designed by golf architect Alfred H. Tull. Near St. George's is the eighteen-hole, well-manicured St. George's Golf Club Course, also laid out by Robert Trent Jones, the newest in Bermuda.

TREASURE DIVING

Tales to delight a dreaming boy are told of treasure diving round Bermuda. Between pirates and storms, ships bearing fortunes undoubtedly were sunk in these waters. What the treasure hunter looks for when he explores undersea with SCUBA outfit or by helmet diving are ballast rocks and straight lines. The ballast rocks are piles of river-washed stone, obviously out of place in the sea and often all that is visible of an old sunken ship. The straight lines may mean cannon or keels, for the sea is not given to forming straight lines naturally. Today experienced divers scan the water around Bermuda with metal-detecting devices and by eye from helium balloons and small aircraft flying low and slow.

Teddy Tucker, born in Paget, Bermuda, in 1925, is living proof that treasure can be found. In his youth he became a profi-

The Sessions House in Hamilton

cient diver and in World War II the Royal Navy found good use for his proficiency. He went into commercial diving in 1949, and in 1955 he came up with a magnificent gold and emerald cross from the Spanish ship **San Pedro,** lost on Bermuda's north reefs in the fall of 1594. Since then the sea has given up more than a million dollars' worth of treasure to him from wrecks of the past four centuries. Treasure divers today comb the archives of Europe for clues as to what sank where and when. The nice thing about undersea treasure hunting off Bermuda is that the day is not lost when you find nothing—the scenery is so beautiful.

The 350th Anniversary of Bermuda's Parliament

In 1970 Bermuda pridefully celebrated the 350th anniversary of the Bermuda Parliament, the first Parliament in the western world, and the oldest in the present world next to those of Britain and Iceland. The islanders have taken to heart the dictum "Mankind has two alternatives: Free and orderly discussion in Parliament with majority rule or fighting in the streets."

The first self-government in Bermuda was carried on by a House of Assembly, which first met in 1620 after the burgesses had sworn an oath that they would transact their business with impartiality and "due secrecy." This first Parliament passed fifteen bills, made plans to build bridges, protect wild life, inspect tobacco, and hold assizes twice a year to punish criminals. The governor, appointed by the Adventurers of the Virginia Company who had founded the colony, presided, and the company approved all the initial laws. This first Parliament met on August 1, 1620, in St. Peter's Church in St. George's. In the same year the building of a Sessions House, now the oldest structure on the islands, began. Rough-cut limestone blocks two feet thick were used for the walls, and they were cemented together with a mortar made of lime and turtle oil.

When the capital of Bermuda was moved to Hamilton from St. George's in 1815, the House of Assembly first met in the Customs House Warehouse. This was built in 1794, and its most recent role has been as a fire station. A new Sessions House was completed on a crest overlooking the harbor in 1826. It is still part of the larger

Gen.Sir John Henry Lefroy
K.C.M.G., C.B., F.R.S., R.A.
Governor of Bermuda 1871-1877

Lt.Gen.Sir T.L. Gallway, K.C.M.G.
Governor of Bermuda 1882-1888

Sessions House in which Parliament meets today. Two old pieces of statuary that once graced Westminster Palace walls and a heraldic lion from Britain stand at the entrance to the Sessions House. The Assembly meets on the second floor and the Supreme Court on the first floor. The Speaker's gavel used today was made from Bermuda cedar and used in the first Assembly meeting in 1620.

Initially it was required that to qualify to vote a citizen must own one share (twenty-five acres) of the Bermuda Company. This was soon changed to require ownership of land valued at two hundred pounds or more. Only men over twenty-one were entitled to vote. Parliamentary elections were held over a three-day period to allow all voters time to travel to the polling places in their parishes.

Bermuda's Government Today

Women were given the right to vote in 1944. In 1963 a Parliamentary Election Act gave the voting privilege to everyone over the age of twenty-five and allowed property owners an extra, or "plus", vote. This act was amended in 1966 when every citizen of Bermuda twenty-one years old or older was enfranchised and the plus vote was eliminated. British subjects who have resided on the islands for three years or more can also vote.

Today the islands are governed under the Constitution of 1968. The governor, appointed by the Crown for a term of three to five years, is the Commander-in-Chief of Bermuda. Bermuda's Parliament consists of a lower house, the House of Assembly, and a upper house, the Senate. Members of the House of Assembly are elected. The governor must then send for the majority party leader, the Premier, and ask him to form a government. The Premier recommends the members of the Cabinet and they are formally appointed by the governor. The Senate is also composed of members appointed by the governor, five on the advice of the Premier, three on the advice of the leader of the next largest party in the Assembly, and three independents chosen by the governor alone.

The constitution contains a Bill of Rights protecting the basic rights and freedoms of individuals. The Civil Service is a nonpolitical body. There is a Supreme Court of Bermuda, from which appeals may be taken to the Court of Appeal for Bermuda. Minor offenses and traffic violations are tried in two lower courts over which magistrates preside.

THE RAILWAY TRAIL

Bermuda had a brief flirt with railways. A narrow-gauge rail line was built in the 1920s linking the entire island, and gasoline engines pulled small trains from one small station (often a corrugated iron shack) to another. In 1945 it was decided that the cost of repairing the railway after the Second World War, when maintenance had been deferred, was too great, and the tracks and rolling stock were sold to Guyana while the bus system was instituted instead.

The right-of-way was neglected for many years, except in Southampton and Somerset, where a walking, cycling and equestrian path demonstrated a beneficial use. Finally Bermuda took up the challenge, and completed, as far as possible, «The Railway Trail». The Trail is mostly reserved for walkers, horse-back riders and pedal cyclists, and provides a level pathway (apart from dips and diversions where bridges were) to enjoy a close-up acquaintance with Bermuda. Here and there are beautiful views across the water, while in other places the route passes through leafy tunnels in stretches of woodland. Part of the trail has a tarred finish, while other sections are sandy paths.

Pamphlets describing the Trail, as well as other walks, are available.

Envoi

The land, the sea, and the air of Bermuda are saturated with a very special and individual beauty. The history of the islands enhances their charm and reveals that the great events of olden days did not pass this land by. Bermuda was very much involved in wars, blockade running, privateering, submarine pursuit. But for a long time now, the economy has been based on a most peaceful and pleasant industry—playing host to visitors. Time does not dim Bermuda's charms for tourists, because Bermudians bring to the art of hospitality such long experience.

Index

Index of Color Pictures

Index of Black & White Pictures

N
W
E
S
SEA GARDENS
MARITIME MUSEUM AND DOCKYARD
IRELAND ISLAND NORTH
THE CUT BRIDGE
IRELAND ISLAND SOUTH
GRASSY BAY
CAMBRIDGE BEACHES
DANIEL'S HEAD
MANGROVE BAY
SOMERSET VILLAGE
WATFORD I.
WATFORD BRIDGE
SANDYS
STOVELL BAY
SPANISH POINT
DEEP BAY
CAVELLO BAY
SOMERSET ISLAND
PEMBROKE
North Shore
QUE
ELY'S HARBOUR
FORT SCAUR
GREAT SOUND
WRECK HILL
DEV
SOMERSET BRIDGE
HAWKINS I.
Hamilton
THE PRINCESS
HAMILTON HARBOUR
BOTANI GARDE
Middle Road
MINSON I.
GRACE I.
DARRELL I.
BELMONT HOTEL & GOLF CLUB
Harbour Road
PAGET
BURGESS POINT
RIDDELL'S BAY GOLF & COUNTRY CLUB
Middle Road
Little Sound
SOUTHAMPTON PRINCESS & GOLF CLUB
South Road
WEST WHALE BAY
WARWICK
ELBOW BEACH
CORAL BEACH
SOUTHAMPTON
DISCOVERY BAY BEACH
MERMAID BEACH
HIGH POINT
CHURCH BAY
THE REEFS
SONESTA BEACH
JOBSON COVE
HORSESHOE BAY
PRINCESS BEACH CLUB
GIBB'S HILL LIGHTHOUSE
Atl